THIS IS IRAQ

Beyond a Thousand and One Words

DEBORAH L. WILLIAMS

in collaboration with

PETER D. MUSGROVE

Copyright © 2023 Deborah L. WILLIAMS

All rights reserved.

ISBN: 9798852908889

To the people of Iraq
Resilient, positive,
generous and welcoming,
you are an inspiration.
Thank you.

CONTENTS

	Acknowledgments	i
	Map of Iraq with places visited	ii
1	Prologue	1
2	Baghdad	7
3	Karbala, Najf, and Kufa	45
4	Babylon	61
5	Nasiriyah, Ziggurat of Ur, and The Marshes	71
6	Basrah	89
7	Samarra	103
8	Ctesiphon	113
9	Erbil	127
10	Mosul	145
11	Epilogue	159
	About Peter	163
	Captions and Photo Credits	164
	About the Author	167

ACKNOWLEDGMENTS

Many thanks to Nick Cornwall for the photo of us Flying High on the Ziggurat, page 81, and for the laughs and good company along the way.
Nick Cornwall Photography
www.nickcornwall.com

And a huge thank you to Xavier for his advice, ideas and patient help in creating the book cover and interior.

Map of Iraq with places visited

1

PROLOGUE

In the chill of a March morning in the French Pyrenees, with fresh snow on the mountains, driving rain, and intermittent howling gales, my mind flees to thoughts of elsewhere, and as on a magic carpet, I fly away.

This time my memories whisk me back to the deserts of Iraq in the autumn of 2022 - memories of heat, dust and unplanned roaming through ancient sites, magical moments and encounters with a people of such warm welcomes and hospitality that I am still reeling from the experience.

My diary notes are shockingly scanty, but take me instantly back to those days of treading carefully through ancient Sumerian sites, discovering an ancient city I had never before heard of, avoiding razor wire, landmines and casually meandering through Baghdad's lawless traffic. A smile lightens my face as I recall the richly warm welcomes of the people I met, their humour and resilience, and once again I am humbled.

*

Back in late August 2022 I read an article on the BBC, about the Ziggurat of Ur, an ancient marvel of Iraq. I had never heard of it. Photos of the Ziggurat rising from the desert sands enthralled me, and searching the internet I learned it was now easy to get visas for Iraq, so promptly wrote to my friend Peter. Let's go! he replied, recalling his visit to Iraq thirty years ago, of dancing the night away in the After Eight Club and being driven through Baghdad's early morning streets on a wild search for a hamburger. He vividly remembers the hand of a policeman on his shoulder in front of the Rafidain Bank and, accused of spying, spending time in the custody of the competent authorities. And then there were the convoys of military hardware trundling through the midnight streets of Baghdad on their way to the Kuwaiti border, for this was in the days just before the invasion of Kuwait. Buying Iraqi dinar in Kuwait at ten times the official rate he smuggled it into the country in his shoes. Iraq was cheap, and he paid $1 a night for a hotel complete with resident rat. Those were the days. I wanted to go.

*

At the beginning of October Peter and I rendezvoused in Amman where I was sure we'd get reliable information on the safety of travelling in Iraq. But most Jordanians advised against it. Too dangerous. At our hotel we met a Christian businessman from Duhok in Kurdistan, who spoke of the numerous militias and their unpredictable behaviour. He didn't encourage us to go.

The UK, French and Australian Embassies all warned against travel there. What to do? Who to believe? Over the next few weeks we to-and-froed between shall we? or shall we not? It seemed that we were on a foolhardy mission. I was full of hesitation, but Peter wasn't. He was determined to go, so undaunted we went to the Iraq Embassy, fronted by a joyful blue replica of the Ishtar Gate, to enquire about visas. Not possible at the Embassy, they said, only on arrival, as hands flapped towards the invisible distance. At the land border? A vague 'yes' was all they could offer. And visa fees? We were brushed off with noncommittal replies. They didn't know. We left more confused than when we had arrived, though were cheered up by the excited little man working at the reception counter. Bubbling with energy and impressive efficiency it was his job to take all mobile phones from visitors, but he also reassured us that Iraq is a wonderful country and all would be well. He was such a bright and positive spark of joy that he made me want to go to Iraq all the more. So with airfares deemed too expensive, the search began for a shared taxi from Amman to Baghdad. We roamed the Abdali *servees*[1] taxi station which lines two sides of a busy road, comparing different information regarding timings and prices until we decided that a large man sitting calmly in front of his Taxi office was the most sincere. No money upfront, just the name of our hotel and the driver would

---

[1] *Servees* taxis are shared taxis, and leave when full. They roam on specific routes all over Amman and also do longer trips to Damascus, Beirut and Baghdad

pick us up at 4.00 AM. And so it was settled. We booked seats in the taxi for the following day.

It was with perversity and a certain trepidation that we made the decision to visit a country whose history and culture had long intrigued me. But off we went, braving the long desert road, towards an eternity of checkpoints and into a land layered with the remnants of war. And where nothing would be as expected.

*

Here then is my tribute to a country and her people, much maligned in western media, but in reality a culture rich in lessons we can all learn much from.

***

At the Iraq Border

Dome in old souq, Baghdad

We deserve life, on Sadoun Street

2

BAGHDAD

Baghdad – founded in 762 AD and known as Madinat as-Salaam, the City of Peace - was once a centre of learning and culture. Graced with magnificent mosques, madrasahs[2] and palaces, for around 500 years it was considered one of the greatest cities in the world.

Alas no longer - fractured by wars, revolts and uprisings for much of the past 100 years, its streets now glitter with shattered glass, its old houses speak of faded grandeur as they crumble and collapse, razor wire spills out from tangled gardens and walls, and the constant threat of collapsing buildings sends you veering out into the traffic. Roads and bridges are blocked by huge slabs of blast-proof concrete while military in full battle gear man endless security checkpoints.

*

Nothing remains of Baghdad's early golden days, but there is enough from later eras to tease the imagination –

---

[2] An educational institute – religious or secular

stunning blue domed mosques, the sturdy remains of an ancient city gate, statues of Scheherazade, Ali Baba, and a magic carpet…. Amongst the rubble and the rubbish are tantalising glimpses of the past. Like double or triple exposures you must sift through the damage to appreciate the curlicued balconies of old houses on Al Rasheed Street, cream brick walls of old madrasahs inlaid with delicate blue tiles. Look up and see the time-tinged brick domes inlaid with blue in an old souq, and you know, you see, you feel the past which once was.

In search of ancient places we wandered back streets lined with shops specialising in car parts and metal work, the air thick with dust, dust, dust. We followed lanes with open drains, and lined with homes so close they almost touched overhead, past the rotting tangle of ancient *shanasheel*[3] work on old homes, past once green squares now turned into car parks, and along muddy paths best avoided. We saw the old, the new, the mess and the beauty, and the lives the people live.

*

Monday 24 October 2022: Waiting for an early morning pick up from the New Park Hotel in Amman, Peter and I were sitting blearily in the lobby when on the dot of 3.30 AM a well dressed, middle-aged man emerged from the staircase and sauntered cheerily towards us. Bright-eyed, hair neatly cut, trimmed moustache, and wearing a smart knitted vest he summoned us with a soft smile and a perky 'Yallah'. Let's go. 'Baghdad?' we queried,

---

[3] Also called *Mashrabiya* – protruding wooden latticework window

and with a nod from our driver off we went, down the stairs, into a waiting GMC[4], and on through the dark and empty early morning streets of Amman. Stopping along the way to pick up two other passengers, a well-fed doctor and a silent Iraqi youth who snuggled into the luggage on the back seat, we headed east on the Zarqa road, pausing for the driver to pray at a mosque on a desolate stretch while we waited, whipped by a cold wind. Onward and into the deep orange hues of a desert sunrise casting its morning light on a flat, dry landscape of stones, rocks, boulders and swathes of smooth sand glowing red and gold.

Five and a half hours later we drove through the archway marking the Iraqi border. It was 9.30 AM and the Foreign Counter was closed, but we were curtly grilled by a tall, abrupt and terrifying major. Why? Where? How long in Iraq? He threw questions at us like a Gatling gun, striking fear into our souls before we were ushered into an office furnished with a comfortable couch and armchairs, and told to wait. An Iraqi flag was on display, and the wall behind the desk was graced with a gold-framed 3D picture of galleons sailing the high seas, an unusual choice in the middle of the desert.

Tea with a hint of cardamom, Iraqi style, was courteously served as we waited for the curt major to re-appear. When he finally arrived he was clutching a plastic folder from which he drew a sheaf of visa application forms, a bundle of visas to be pasted into passports, and assorted pens and stamps. After carefully

[4] GMCs are SUV vehicles seating up to seven passengers

and slowly arranging all in an orderly fashion on his desk, he grilled us again about our visit to Iraq. Peter was then summoned to write his details in English on the visa application form, and the major's fierce face transformed into a naughty grin when the question of male or female / man or woman arose. In an outburst of joyful exuberance our major declared loudly that 'women are beautiful, very beautiful' and his beaming smile broadened further each time he uttered the word 'beautiful'. 'Me, or all women?' I asked, and now he was guffawing while Peter and I dissolved into uncontrolled giggles. It would have continued had not a young Chinese woman arrived with another official, whereupon the serious curtness returned in a flash to our major's face.

An hour later, visas safely pasted into passports with our own fair hands, and visa-fee receipts issued, we were free to leave. We didn't know it then, but we had been issued a mysterious receipt for money we hadn't paid, provoking a later flurry of calls between border post and our driver who insisted he would have to pay the unpaid fee next time he passed the border. A dispute erupted about the exact amount we owed - from minuscule to a lot - and it was only when we arrived in Baghdad and gave him a healthy tip that we convinced him the amount was minuscule. Terrified that we would be nabbed at the border later on when leaving from Erbil, we photographed all receipts.

In our naivete we assumed it would now be a quick five hour run to Baghdad, but no. As we sped down the flat desert road lined with small forts and bunkers fortified by concrete slabs, dirt and rubble, past carcasses of burnt-out cars, trucks and buses, and under sandbagged bridges, we were halted at military checkpoint after checkpoint, our passports carefully perused, and we were questioned by soldiers in full battle gear. At one long checkpoint a masked soldier with stunning eyes and good English questioned us, and in an absurd effort to normalise the situation I pointed to a massive dog lying on a pile of sand. 'Look, there's a dog,' said I, inanely. 'He is sleeping.' What on earth was I thinking? But Mr Handsome Eyes played along with the game and his sparkling eyes most definitely lightened the long wait. In a delightful moment of confusion, checkpoint soldiers lined us up for a photo as we smiled gaily for the camera assuming this was just a friendly snap. It was in fact a photo to be forwarded down the line of checkpoints for identification.

Of the many checkpoints between the Jordan-Iraq border and Baghdad, we endured at least five major ones, of which two took seemingly forever. Soldiers in full military kit, masked faces, helmets topped with night cameras, and AK47s at the ready, took our passports, made mysterious phone calls and kept us waiting for up to 45 minutes at each checkpoint. And the road went on and on as we passed mini-forts surrounded by neatly painted stones, and lookout towers like mini lighthouses painted in red, white and black stripes. Forts and walls were covered with Allahu Akbar written in swirling Arabic, and bombed bridges and buildings, now mere piles of rubble and concrete slabs lurching at impossible angles flashed by.

At the first checkpoint the soldiers had wanted to escort us to the next one, for our safety, but no vehicle was available. They were well-meaning but had little or no experience of foreigners arriving by road and were reluctant to take the responsibility of letting us continue. At the final checkpoint before Baghdad the novelty had worn off and an inkling of what it must feel like to be held hostage began to creep in. Thirty minutes passed before a lanky, red-arm-banded soldier cheerily gave us the thumbs up, and we were farewelled with the sweetest 'Bye-bye, until we meet again!' from a burly, flirtatious soldier.

Our patience was fraying badly but there was nothing to do. Not long before Baghdad the doctor in the front seat quietly turned his head, saying 'This is Fallujah', as he nodded towards a town edged with new buildings under construction. A little further on he muttered something about 'a prison'. It was the infamous Abu Ghraib prison and he clearly assumed that we knew of the horrors which had unfolded in both Fallujah and Abu Ghraib. Which we did. In the solemn silence which followed, discussion was not necessary. His voice said it all. And to be honest, what can you say? Words quite simply aren't there. It was a sobering moment, and knowing what had happened in these two places, how could we even think of whinging about our checkpoint hold ups.

Arriving at the perimeter of Baghdad there was one final checkpoint, a claustrophobic and chaotic vision of hell, as heaving traffic was channelled slowly between towering vertical slabs of red and yellow striped blast-proof concrete, narrowly hemming us in on either side, while black uniformed men led powerful dogs past the cars and trucks, checking for explosives and to no doubt intimidate. Engines roared, fumes belched. Voices shouted above the commotion. This was a monster checkpoint, a legacy of the Americans, we were told, and within those concrete slabs, noise and filthy air, it retained all the horrific vibrations of the war. It was a feeling of horror I felt nowhere else in Iraq.

So it was a huge relief to move on and finally judder into Baghdad's major traffic jams at around 5.30 PM, and by the time we were dropped at the Diwan Hotel on Sadoun Street the trip had taken more than 14 long hours. Our driver was clearly shattered though remained stoically calm and had not once complained about the long waits at the security checks. He was a man who had lived through worse moments, he knew things we couldn't imagine, and he deserved a medal.

Welcomed at the hotel by an arrogant young receptionist, and shown a depressing room with a filthy bathroom was not exactly a good start to Baghdad. Neither of us had the energy to look for a better option for the night, but at least we were no longer battling security checkpoints.

That first night in Baghdad, despite the grimy state of our room I slept well, though woke during the night to the sound of rustling paper. Shooting upright in bed and crying out 'There's a rat!', quick off the mark I shone my torchlight towards the sound and onto a terrified Peter who froze while scrabbling in the dark looking for panadol to ease his toothache. The memory still has the power to send me into shaking laughter.

If the Diwan's room was dire, its breakfast, served in a cavernous dining room with a leaking ceiling and stalagmites forming on the floor, was excellent. We downed the traditional Iraqi lentil soup, cauliflower, aubergine and excellent flat bread until bursting point. Few other guests shared the dining room save for some VERY fierce bodyguard types! The dining and kitchen staff were Yezidi from Kurdistan, bouncy young men with character and warm smiles. Later we would discover that many hotel staff in Iraq were Syrian, Lebanese, Pakistani, Kurdish, and all were delightful.

*

Few signs in English announced the presence of hotels on Sadoun Street, and though I know the Arabic word for hotel, unable to read Arabic I was lost. Fortunately Peter does read Arabic, so after breakfast, in and out of different hotels we went, looking at rooms and having mad encounters along the way. We met young men clad in nightclub style sparkling clothes, rode in a lift which, judging by the layers of clogged rubbish between doors and lift on each floor, had seen no maintenance for years. We were invited several times to join the staff as they downed their breakfast, and one reception desk had a nifty daily-date contraption showing April July 22, when it should have been October 25. Not that it mattered.

At another hotel we became friendly with Adel, the dapper Lebanese receptionist who also doubled as a money changer, offering good rates. In another life he'd been a nightclub singer until losing his voice with too many cigarettes. He was always immaculately dressed in smart shirts, stove pipe trousers, and perfectly polished shoes, and without fail entertained us with tales, and between cigarettes, huskily crooned love songs in Arabic.

Another Lebanese singer occasionally worked there - his hair swept up and sprayed into a work of art after his daily visit to his coiffeur. Dressed smartly and entirely in black, and hyper bubbly, he excitedly talked about the women in Lebanon as he flourished and tore at his matching black prayer beads. He was in Iraq because there was electricity, and worked as a singer in the evenings. He'd been around in his short life, and in rapid English peppered with obscenities he claimed that US $50 would buy time with a girl in Dubai. Lurching from wild tales to a moment of wild singing, he flourished his spiky purple hairbrush as a microphone before we retreated back out to the street.

Finally we found a small hotel with an aura of respectability despite the number of men slouching in a haze of smoke in the lobby. The Dijlat al-Khair offered us a room with turquoise decor and curtains to match, and an oddly placed large white pillar adorned with great black polka dots. Idly standing behind it one morning I stunned Peter who thought I had suddenly vanished. Beds had two sheets - not always the norm in a part of the world where hotels are often classified according to the number of sheets on beds - and a towel had to be purchased for extra dinar. Not a problem. We liked it, and checked in.

The room boys were from Pakistan and downstairs we met Radi, a tall, lean Syrian in charge of the breakfast room. He was an angel, dashing out to buy Peter cloves – delightfully named *harumpfel* in Arabic - for his toothache, and refusing payment. He provided a running commentary on the silent, bucolic scenes of Syria unfolding on the morning television, joked about his hangover from a night out drinking on the street, made faces behind surly unsociable guests, and was all in all a delight. No doubt he'd been a bad lad in his time and had a history, but we liked him.

*

That first day, heading out towards the old Shabandar Cafe on Mutanabbi Street, we walked straight into blocked and barricaded roads where military police were thick on the ground. After the previous day's endless checkpoints I assumed this was just another typical day in Baghdad, but no, a demonstration marking the anniversary of the 2019 October Protest Movement, or the Tishreen Movement, was swelling with protesters at nearby Tahrir Square[5]. Stopped by the military police who politely asked to see our passports, we were told we could continue, but advised against it.

[5] Liberation Square, in English, in the centre of Baghdad

Possible encounters with tear gas or live bullets didn't really appeal, so we walked away from the demonstration and the ever advancing troops of soldiers in blue, stopping briefly to watch two men peacefully playing backgammon on the pavement before meandering on through Abu Nuwas Park which stretches along the banks of the Tigris.

Peter remembers when you could walk on pleasant paths there and eat fish at small eateries or sip tea in a cafe in the evening. Now the cafes and eateries have gone, replaced by piles of bulldozed sand and silt blocking access to the river bank, lots of razor wire and possibly an unexploded device. You never know. Come late afternoon the homeless and alcoholics gather there. Rubbish and shattered glass lined the paths.

So we paused at a small tea stall by the roadside, overlooking the greenery of the park, and with our spirits soaring we sipped *chai*[6] laced with cardamom, unexpectedly paid for by the Iraqi men who perched next to us on a rug-covered low-lying wall. 'This is Iraq', they insisted, roaring their refusal to let us pay. Our first encounter with the extraordinary hospitality of Iraqis.

We spent that first day just wandering, passing once stylish houses in side-streets and sculptures from A Thousand and One Nights, of Scheherazade, a flying carpet, Sindbad the Sailor.

That evening we dined on excellent liver sandwiches in a small, hole-in-the-wall sandwich shop near Tahrir Square not far from the demonstration. Peter and I sat at

[6] Tea

a counter happily munching our sandwiches when a troop of tired, hungry soldiers invaded the shop. We were suddenly surrounded by military, fully armed, guns and batons hanging from their muscled bodies, and I have a vivid memory of one soldier with a black rubber mask in the shape of a blank face hanging on his back. I've always thought it unwise to hang out with soldiers, but there we were, surrounded by them in a small space, and instead of fear, I was totally fascinated. Peter recalls a series of selfies taken of us with the soldiers.

*

Never knowing what would happen next, even buying a sim card was a joyful adventure. On Sadoun Street we found a Zain phone shop with all the latest phones and accessories, and managed by the efficient Youssuf Muhammad who helped me to choose and buy a sim card before finally insisting on videoing us repeating after him, in Arabic, 'I love you Youssuf Muhammad!' He was genuinely thrilled to have foreign customers and we were delighted to oblige with repeated renditions of 'We love you Youssuf Muhammad'. Alas, I cannot remember the Arabic for what we said. I can also not imagine this happening in a western shop!

The following day, with the demonstration at Tahrir Square over and concrete barricades removed, we eventually made it to the Shabandar cafe. Abandoning busy roads we meandered through smaller streets until, arriving at the river, we spontaneously jumped aboard a small ferry which puttered us slowly and peacefully upstream through the Dijlat's[7] silken waters. With the wind in our hair and smiles on our faces, sailing on the Tigris was a moment of timeless magic. As if we were floating through history. Dropped at the bottom of a flight of broken, rubbish strewn steps, we picked our way over muddy rubble and up to Mutanabbi Street, lined with shops and stalls selling books old and new. Here you can take your pick from Anne of Green Gables, Roald Dahl, political tomes, books on advanced science, biographies, children's books and old postcards, while street carts sold freshly squeezed pomegranate juice. The street and buildings have been much restored and at the Tigris end stands a statue of the 10th-century Abbasid era poet Mutanabbi. At the other end, giving on to Al Rasheed Street, is a tall yellow-brick arched entrance.

The Shabandar Cafe, founded in 1917, stands on a corner of Mutanabbi Street, and is still thriving despite a 2007 bomb blast which ripped through the street and cafe, killing many, including five members of the owner's family, and injuring many more. But uncowed, Iraqi resilience has won the battle, so far. Known as a haven for intellectuals and culture, the cafe was crowded, with mostly men, but a few women, seated at tables surrounded by traditional wooden benches covered with colourful Bedu[8] style rugs. The walls were carpeted in black and white photos of old Baghdad, old Iraq, of street scenes, people and ancient monuments.

---

[7] Dijlat is the Arabic name for the Tigris River

[8] Bedouin

Great polished copper samovars stood on shelves amidst the bubble and hazy smoke from *nargillahs*[9]. We shared a table with a smoker who later discreetly vanished, we talked with strangers, a huddle of schoolboys at the next table, and then a poet from Karbala who joined us. Young, handsome, curly haired and with a cheeky, twinkling smile, he was a teacher, wrote Haiku poetry and taught his teenage students via song. He was utterly charming.

But cards and board games are banned at Shabandar, so looking for a cafe where we could play *tawla*[10], we moved on to the Umm Kulthum cafe on Al Rasheed Street, supposedly older than the Shabandar Cafe, grubbier, less pristine and less touristy, and perhaps for that reason, charming in a less contrived way. Its walls were covered with photos of Umm Kulthum, that most famous of Egyptian singers, and recordings of the great singer endlessly filled the air. A young man with hair gelled up and swept back in magnificent Elvis style appeared, as the clack of dominoes, *tawla* and chess pieces competed with Umm Kulthum's crooning. We sat on benches covered in brown vinyl, playing *tawla*, until a self proclaimed 'rich man' - 'I am rice' [sic] - who had worked in Russia as an engineer, sat opposite and flattered me by saying I played *tawla* '*helweh*', beautifully. He insisted on paying for our tea and giving us Pepsi, while another man passed by with a tray of

---

[9] *Nargillah* - a water pipe, hookah, sheesha

[10] Backgammon

buns and *simsim*[11] bread, placing three on our table before distributing the rest to all in the cafe. Never had I experienced such generosity. But this is Iraq. And Umm Kulthum crooned on, her voice rising and falling, filling the space with a soothing peace and passion. Through the haze of *sheesha* smoke her silken voice mingled with the clack of dominoes and murmuring from tables where men, mostly men, old and traditional, conservative, young and trendy, sat. Old tape players and hifi systems long out of use gathered dust on a counter and we played *tawla* on a battered board adorned with elegantly curved niches for holding the counters and a swirling painting of a sensual woman.

Tawla and tea in the Umm Kulthum Cafe

*

---

[11] *Simsim* - sesame

Outside, old buildings crumbled.

Old Baghdad's buildings, once a treasure trove of *shanasheel* or *mashrabiya*, the ornately lattice-worked and enclosed wooden balconies, are collapsing. Still standing buildings often lurch drunkenly at erratic angles as if an earthquake has rumbled by, and down the alleyways beyond the Umm Kulthum cafe there are ancient metal studded gates, arched doorways, and sturdier brick structures which hint at the past. The ruins of an old *hammam* protruded from dust and rubble, occasional turquoise pieces stared out from remnants of ornate brickwork in old walls, and at the end of an alleyway there occasionally shimmered the glorious turquoise dome of an ancient mosque. We wandered *hinny minny*[12] through a maze of ruins, junk shops and antique dealers, coming across old mugs adorned with Princess Diana's photo, and an Iraqi refugee who'd gone at some point to Syria but was deported back to Iraq. He was desperate to tell his story and would still be talking of his sad life had we not made an escape. We were there on a Friday when an eerie stillness shrouded the area, and perhaps the past spoke louder through the silence. It was like walking in another time zone and being the last survivors... But Baghdad is full of old houses sagging, crumbling and lurching in terrifying lopsided wonder as crowds surge timelessly past, while stunning blue-domed mosques of Persian influence rise serenely beside roads and above the jumble of people and traffic. The city is still, quite simply, magnificent.

[12] *Hinny minny* – Arabic for 'here and there'

Top: Haydar-Khana Mosque on Al Rasheed Street
Bottom: Sagging building in old Baghdad

*

At Tahrir Square we met two teenage schoolboys who were playing truant. They spoke excellent English, and when asked 'Why are the traffic lights red but the cars are not stopping?' they simply replied 'This is Iraq', before asking a policeman to usher us across the busy road. Which he did.

We then blithely embarked on an unforgettably long walk along what must be the noisiest street in the world, Khulafa Street, which we renamed The Street of Babel. Lined with a myriad of shops and stalls, concealed mini loudspeakers shouted the wares of every shop, every cart, and every stall, savaging the air with an earsplitting cacophony until my head was splitting and spinning. It is a street of impenetrable crowds and broken pavements, but through the crowded, watch-your-step pirouetting throngs we went, past food, nuts, plumbing supplies and car parts, until the crowds thinned, the noise eased and we stopped, delirious, at a street corner drink-cart where a blackish-brown drink was on offer. It was not an appealing sight, but we were desperate, and joy of joys, it was divine. Made from dried black limes it was called 'noomi basra'. And despite our protests the vendor refused payment. This is Iraq.

When we arrived in Iraq we had vowed to avoid crowded places, popular targets of suicide bombers, but Khulafa Street well and truly put paid to our naive plan, and in fact set the scene for further fearless forays into the midst of masses. You could say that Khulafa Street broke the ice of fear.

*

Clouds of feathery dusters were for sale on Al Rasheed Street which runs in a straight line through the old part of town. Once an elegant strip lined with fine architecture, it is now in an appalling state. Here there are remnants of Baghdad's more recent glory, from the early 20th century when it began as an Ottoman military road, running parallel to the Tigris and providing access to docked ships. In 1917 it was the first street in Baghdad to have electric street lighting, and cinemas and cafes appeared for the benefit of military officers. The British in their turn introduced nightclubs and orchestras, musical entertainment flourished and during the 1940s and 50s shops selling luxury goods were overlooked by the curvaceous balconies and windows of stylish homes.

But Al Rasheed Street was not only a nightlife hotspot and scene of the good times. It saw violent anti-British protests in 1920, and by the 1980s neglect was beginning to take its toll. The 2003 invasion didn't help and more recently, in 2019 when Baghdadi youth fought running street battles there with government forces, buildings were torched and further damage done to a street already suffering from neglect.

Shops still occupy the ground level, but above that the buildings are often ghostly shells, often bereft of their uppermost floors of which only crenellated balcony ironwork remains. Leaning in all directions, the rows of buildings are held together by little more than a tangle of ancient wiring and the support of newer concrete structures preventing total collapse.

In a city as militarised as Baghdad, it came as no surprise to stumble, late one afternoon, upon a little shop off Al Rasheed Street specialising in militaria. An assortment of military hats stacked on shelves included, oddly, a metal helmet with Viking horns. Berets and caps in sombre shades adorned the decapitated heads of mannequins lining the shelves along one wall, while a startling array of bandoliers, gun holsters and desert boots attracted the eye of potential customers. A particularly intimidating cadaverous dummy sported a flak jacket, helmet and dark glasses and would have instilled fear in the heart of any enemy on the battlefield or elsewhere. But our eyes were drawn to something else in the shop: there, on the second shelf, amid the military headgear, was a spotlit model sporting the most incongruous scarlet feathered, sequinned and gilded winged mask, as perfect for the Carnivale in Venice as if it had been fabricated for just such an occasion. Disappointingly, during all our time in Iraq and at the many checkpoints that we subsequently passed through, we never once encountered a soldier sporting anything remotely similar to this frivolous confection, though it would certainly have brightened our day if we had.

By day a myriad of street stalls do loud and lively business along the gutters and under covered walkways which are overhung by crumbling plaster and supported by battered columns. Hanging at a jaunty, lopsided angle from the ceiling of one of these walkways was a large poster of Mr Bean looking down onto piles of discarded cardboard boxes with a mad grin on his face.

Here, evenings were once vibrant with cinema goers, music and *sheesha* smokers in cafes, but now, come 4.00 PM it has become a no-go zone. Wandering home at 3.00 PM just as stall holders were packing up their goods, we were advised to get out as it was dangerous. Why was it dangerous, I asked. No enlightening reply came back. It's just dangerous. Looking down the narrow poorly lit alleys leading off Al Rasheed Street I was not surprised, for behind the once fine facades, the dank rubbish filled alleys could only be home to desperate souls, and quite possibly ISIS[13]. Who knows.

But magically, the past elegance still lingers softly through the mess.

Military apparel fit for the Carnivale

---

[13] ISIS – Islamic State, also known as IS, ISIL and Daesh

Mr Bean gazing down on Al Rasheed Street

*

Al Rasheed street was not the only place we were warned to leave. Late one afternoon, walking back from Tahrir Square we wandered into a side street and were confronted with an apocalyptic vision of old houses decaying amongst garbage, pieces of wood hanging like flimsily attached shards, holes gaping in walls which had once given comfortable shelter. Debris, rubbish and dank pools of waste water filled the street, not totally unlike other side-streets in Baghdad, but something here was very wrong. It reeked of bad energy. It was here that a man stopped us, urging us to leave, the street was dangerous, bad people lived there. Thieves? Remnants of ISIS? We didn't question, just thanked him and left, stepping past a makeshift road block, and as through a looking glass, back into the normalcy of Sadoun Street.

Apocalyptic side-street off Sadoun Street

And not far away the Tigris flows timelessly on and on and on, as ferry boats, small and large, take locals and day-trippers up, down and across the river.

*

Peter's tooth had been causing him much pain since Jordan, munching on cloves no longer helped, and by our third day in Baghdad the tooth had become so painful that he agreed to be led to the dental hospital behind the 17 Ramadan Mosque at Firdos Square. It was a government clinic, with pink walls, white tiles, and clean. A young male dentist checked Peter's mouth, and declared there was no cavity. An older female dentist joined in, asking Peter if he was diabetic before declaring that in fact he had a large cavity. We had no idea who to believe, but they both agreed that his teeth needed descaling, and antibiotics were necessary for temporary relief. The check-up was free, but for further care he would have to go to the young man's clinic later that day, and so we left. No fee. This is Iraq.

That afternoon we walked through backstreets lined with more expensive homes safely hidden behind tall walls, over a bridge crossing the Baghdad-Mosul Highway, to the Dream City Mall, an almost shocking, totally out-of-place bastion of shiny, Singapore-style materialism, and on to the nearby dental clinic of Dr Safaa. For US $25 Peter had his teeth carefully cleaned and was entertained for a good hour by tales of the doctor's family life. Dr Safaa insisted on photographing Peter's descaled teeth after the treatment, and Peter is still wondering if they are now beaming from a signboard or in one of the clinic's brochures. All the while I sat on a plush blue velvet armchair in the waiting room. By the time we left the clinic darkness had fallen and as we retraced our steps, crossing over the highway bridge we passed a security checkpoint, and were astonished to hear a soldier excitedly calling out

'*Fransa, Brittania*'. Somewhere during the previous few days this soldier had met us, perused our passports and remembered us. It was astonishing. It was also a reminder that no matter where we went, we were known.

Walking home on Sadoun Street we stopped for a plate of falafel and salad served by a starry-eyed young man at street-side tables. As we ate, a gang of rollerblading Baghdadi youth flew by, wildly weaving their way between cars and flying like black cheetahs when lulls opened in the traffic. By dark of night and clad in black they were living life dangerously, to the max, and loving every minute of it. Next door young *shebab*[14] had their hair arranged into explosively high 'electric-shock' hairstyles in a pricey salon, and further on a shop window displayed the latest men's fashion of tops and trousers swirling with silver sequins like the starry night sky. The ultimate bling. Liberace would have loved it.

As we picked our way along a darker stretch of Sadoun Street, a large shape emerged from the gloom of a darkened doorway, and with ghostly white robes flowing, headed straight for us. He was a giant, and a seller of traditional coffee poured from a voluptuously curved coffee pot into small porcelain cups. Refusal was impossible. The coffee was excellent. And payment out of the question.

However, not every evening encounter was such a delight. We frequently ended the evening with a

[14] Youth, (plural), young men, though I have also used it to describe a single youth.

bedtime carrot or pomegranate juice from a juice shop near the hotel, and one evening were walking back, passing under some poorly lit trees when soldiers asked to see our passports. Nothing unusual about that, but when one of them furtively asked for $100 we were at first astonished, then incensed at this brazen demand for *baksheesh*. In a flash we clutched our passports, and screaming in unison LA! LA! LA! LA! LA! (NO! NO! NO! in Arabic), bolted, running like rockets and not looking back until well clear. From that moment we prudently avoided dark places and made long detours to avoid police checks, if possible.

*

After one of our rambling wanderings, one afternoon we crossed the Shuhada Bridge to the west bank of the Tigris, walking through an area of back street shops selling fishing equipment, and past giant round barbecue pits edged with carp being slowly roasted by red hot coals. We continued along Allawi Street, lined with greying buildings and a mishmash of eateries and shops. Fluffy-feather-footed roosters strutted in roadside gutters, at liberty amongst the mayhem – a not unusual sight in Baghdad. Passing the window of a cake-pastry-biscuit-pudding shop we were instantly taken by the sight of plastic cups filled with yellow custard and red raspberry jelly topped with shavings of pink chocolate. It could only be a relic from the British era, certainly not your usual Iraqi sweet, but when the desire for a creamy dessert tempted, this was the place to go. We were totally seduced, and during our time in Baghdad returned again and again to indulge, walking kilometres and kilometres for the pleasure. There were always customers to chat to and on one occasion we met a tiny Kurdish man who was over the moon to meet us. He was like a little gremlin, straight out of the Lord of the Rings, bright eyed and bubbly, but alas his English was totally incomprehensible. We left him happily burbling in the street, and with custard and jelly in hand walked on towards the Baghdad Train Station. Peter gobbled his as we walked, I finished mine off as we perched on a wall in front of the grand station, happily swinging our legs as traffic hurtled past with horns honking and shouts of 'Welcome to Iraq' from passing shared taxis, followed by a convoy of armour-plated trucks rumbling north.

The Baghdad Train Station

The exterior of the British built Baghdad Train Station verges on severe, but the interior is majestic, soaring, cathedral-like, magnificent. And when we were there, empty.

Cathedral-like interior of the Baghdad Train Station

There were only three trains a week, to Basrah, and nowhere else, and only one window open for purchasing tickets, but according to Wikipedia, when the station opened in the 1950s it offered telegraph services, a bank, post office, saloon, shops and a restaurant. It also had its own printing presses which are apparently still used for printing train tickets today.

After the 2003 invasion it was looted and damaged, but a 2006 renovation restored the building and restaurant, and apparently a 13 room hotel was added. However, I saw no sign of a restaurant or hotel when I was there.

Not far from the station is the impressive Iraq Museum, famously looted during the 2003 invasion. The US did not bomb the museum, but they made no effort to protect it. Nothing at all, and for three days looters plundered and took what they could. One has to loudly ask why one of the few buildings, if not the sole one, not to suffer from looting was the Oil Ministry, which was protected by at least 50 US tanks. The best that Donald Rumsfeld could offer was 'stuff happens'. Really?

The museum, which has now retrieved many of its stolen artefacts, is home to extraordinary pottery from ancient and, to me, unheard of civilisations. Large, airy, and now seemingly well protected, we had an obligatory guide, a young man whose enthusiasm and impressively detailed knowledge of Iraq's history gave hope for the future.

Walking back towards our hotel, on the west side of the Tigris we passed through two strict security checks, a strip of makeshift tents with sprawling soldiers, and then over a bridge heavily fortified with huge blast-proof concrete blocks. Had we inadvertently touched on the Green Zone[15]?

Darkness descended as we continued along a dusty riverside track on the east bank, past gangs of dogs, the wreckage of burned out buses and cars, piled up, abandoned, and a few loitering men. We really shouldn't have been there.

*

Apart from several magnificent mosques and madrasahs, all richly decorated with intricate Persian blue tiles and fine cream brickwork, little remains of Baghdad's ancient days of glory. Of old Baghdad's gates, there is only one which survives, the 12th-century Bab al-Wastani.

Setting forth in search of it, we hadn't gone far before we were halted by great bellows of glee from a burly barber who dashed out of his shop to welcome us to Baghdad. He literally bundled us into his hair salon, sat us down, ordered tea and force fed us with sweets. It was akin to being kidnapped, but in the nicest possible way. He eventually released us and we continued along roads lined with spare car parts and tyres, stopping to visit the 12th-century Mausoleum of Omar Suhrawardi in a dusty cemetery littered with fallen blue tombstone tiles. The mausoleum's tall conical dome is now leaning dangerously and was held aloft within a latticework of protective scaffolding. We moved on, following the street to an impassable overhead highway and from the gloomy space below, we stood amongst rubbish, like

---

[15] Heavily fortified zone, home to government buildings and foreign embassies, also called the International Zone

seedy characters or investigators in a Line of Duty crime scene, viewing the old gate from a distance. It has been much restored, and now fenced off it stands next to the collapsing graves of yet another old cemetery, but an idea of the strength and solidity of the old city walls shines through.

Retracing our steps past car repair workshops we chatted to a young man who was having his 1955 Jaguar restored to its former glory. Different times, different treasures.

Further on we paused in front of the barricaded Latin Cathedral on Khulafa Street and watched as a head-scarfed woman emerged, carrying a large bowl of meat which she distributed carefully, sharing the chunks equally to a band of waiting street dogs. The kindness of people never ceased to move me.

*

Fast forward to the twentieth century. In 1942 my father stayed at the Tigris Palace Hotel overlooking the river. He found it dirty and unpleasant, though old photos show it as a charming two-storey balconied place. Alas, it is now long gone, and by the 1980s concrete skyscraper hotels were sprouting in Baghdad, offering spectacular views over the Tigris and surroundings. At the end of Sadoun Street, on Firdos Square, two of these modern hotels, the Palestine and the Sheraton (now Ishtar) welcomed foreign journalists covering events from the 1991 Gulf War to the 2003 invasion, but unprotected during the 2003 war both suffered damage from rocket fire. The Palestine was shelled by the US military, killing and wounding several journalists, and was later bombed by insurgents in 2005, taking out the lobby. It received a hopeful facelift in 2013 and is still functioning, but eerily quiet, verging on deserted inside. War, bombs and the demise of tourism wreaked the usual damage and by 2022 times had changed.

We stepped into the Palestine Hotel lobby one morning so that Peter could revive his 30-year-old memories of the hotel's happier days, but the only thing he recognised was the Orient Express Restaurant, designed to resemble an old wood-panelled train, elegant and stylish. Its menu boasted an assortment of fish and meat dishes, including Thickness Zubaydi, Chateau Biryani Turnoff, and Sheep Involvement. We resisted the temptation. At that time of day it was empty though a list of reservations suggested it was still popular in the evenings. Sitting in the cool calm of the hotel's cavernous lobby was a welcome retreat from the outside heat, and not without interest as we watched men and the occasional woman who had come along, nervous and dapperly dressed for an all important IELTS exam which might hopefully guarantee a place in a university abroad. A ticket out.

On our last evening in Baghdad we returned to the Palestine to farewell the city with a drink in the 18th floor Panorama Bar which still offers spectacular views over the satiny waters of the Tigris. It was to be our big night out in search of fun. The hotel reception staff were oddly unhelpful when we asked for directions to the Bar, flippantly telling us to take a lift to the top floor. Which we did, only to arrive at the 16th floor and the eeriest of hotel corridors, dimly lit, and clearly uninhabited, abandoned. No sign of a bar, and no sign of a staircase to take us further upwards. Or downwards, for that matter. Imagining the horror of being there if the power failed, my gut feeling was screaming to get out, so back down the lift we went, and were begrudgingly pointed to a hidden service lift which swept us up to the elusive 18th floor. There we were greeted by burly bouncers and unfriendly frowns. Where on earth were we? Feigning confidence, we walked on, past a zombie bouncer strategically seated at a bend in the corridor, on past a room where young women were applying make-up, and into the Panorama Bar, to be confronted by a bevy of working girls, a few male waiters, and a superb view over the sunset tinged Dijlat. Once offering a gay scene to rival any, it is now little more than a prostitutes' bar.

Never mind, perching on bar stools surrounding a sunken serving area, we ordered beers from a young waiter who annoyed Peter by addressing him as 'uncle'. But the moment of grumpiness passed and chatting to him, he spoke of his life, losing his parents and starting work at the age of thirteen. He was now twenty-one and a sweetie, had taught himself enough English to communicate, and dreamed of going to Australia for a better life. Working in this bar was obviously one of the better steps on the path to his dream. Another young man wearing a cowboy hat was mixing drinks in the sunken serving area. His shorter than usual legs meant that his chin barely reached the counter, but he was full of smiles and an exuberant energy and was clearly having fun in his job.

Looking around at the many girls working there, buxom, thin, sexy, plain, aimlessly sashaying, seated alone or in pairs, my eye was caught by an attractive woman dressed soberly in black top and trousers, sitting alone on the far side of the bar. 'Where is that girl from?' I asked, and casting an odd look at me our waiter replied that she was from Turkey, and was not a girl. 'It's a boy,' he said in a lowered voice. A tranny! I wondered how many others she'd fooled. An aggressive and loud Madame arrived to give the girls a dressing down, before they scattered. Two hardened older women sat in a corner drinking and smoking. One pretty young girl, slim and wearing next to nothing, showed maximum flesh, piercing and tattoos, and bubbling with high energy she draped herself over the bar flirting wildly with the waiters. A curvaceous Rubenesque creature, all curls and curves came and smilingly draped herself over both of us, telling us we were beautiful, caressing my arm as she did so and pinching the roll of fat around Peter's girth. He was amused, I was terrified. If she was looking for a threesome, she was out of luck.

The evening wore on, the music became louder, Saudi men in pristine white *thobes*[16] sauntered in, settled into comfortable couches and ordered vast amounts of food and alcohol. The girls now lavished attention on them,

[16] *Thobe* - an ankle length robe, usually long-sleeved, worn by men in Arab countries

abandoning Peter and me. Things were livening up, but by 9.30 PM our solitary and slowly sipped beer glasses were empty, and enough was enough. Saying goodbye to our sweet waiter, and farewelled by the hard-faced ladies, we fled, back down the lift, accompanied this time by friendly bouncers, and out into the streets where a different pick-up scene was unfolding. Sadoun Street had become a night time cruising strip as endless cars lined the dark side of the road, with men, alone or in pairs, waiting, in the front seats. Suspiciously nefarious goings-on were afoot.

Further on, the many alcohol supermarkets on Sadoun Street were doing good business selling genies of pleasure, escape, or whatever, in bottles, mostly spirits, to those who couldn't afford the bars and clubs in dim backrooms behind dark curtains. Cheaper to lurk around car boots where an overtly underground business was in full swing. Finally, I understood the shattered glass lingering and glinting on the pavements.

By the time we'd safely negotiated crossing the busy night-time road, it was a relief to arrive safely back at the hotel. It was only 10.00 PM, but the dark streets of Baghdad's nights had revealed another, seedier world.

The following day, from our room on the fourth floor of the Dijlat al-Khair Hotel, I looked down onto early morning Sadoun Street. A cool young Baghdadi youth sporting a singlet top, shorts and headphones cycled fast in the direction of Firdos Square. Minutes later an elderly man on a rusting, old bike pedalled casually and fearlessly across the traffic, stopping at a small grocery shop opposite our hotel. Slowly and calmly he unloaded boxes of supplies to restock his shop. Young and old, worlds apart, and life goes on. This is Iraq.

*

Despite the mess, the chaos, the tragedy of it all, I fell in love with Baghdad - with the Baghdad of today and the remnants of her yesterday. I fell in love with her often hidden but lingering beauty, and the people, hospitable, welcoming, smiling and kind, resilient and forgiving.

And beyond Baghdad, I fell in love with Iraq, a country riddled with ancient history, beauty, tragedy, occasional danger, and guardian of a tradition of hospitality which has gone missing from our modern westernised world.

***

400-year-old *khan*[17] in souq

[17] Travellers and traders' inn, built around a courtyard

Details on minaret in old Baghdad

Glittering interior of Karbala shrine

3

KARBALA, NAJAF, and KUFA

Karbala, city of holy shrines, shimmering gilded domes and minarets, and oceans of black clad pilgrims. Holy for Shia Muslims, pious, and otherworldly, it lies an hour and a half southwest of Baghdad, reached by a desert highway crisscrossed with traffic hurtling like suicidal dodgem cars at high speed, past fluttering black and green flags, and endless billboards covered with photos of Shia martyrs.

*

We left Baghdad in one of those infernal yellow taxis with a young *shebab* at the wheel, on what proved to be a white knuckle ride to the holy city. It was our first real experience of life on the roads of Iraq, and scarred by the journey from the Jordanian border, Peter tried to diminish his height and girth at each checkpoint while I just draped my scarf over my hair. Not that I fooled anyone.

If the checkpoints weren't stressful enough, from his

middle back-seat vantage point Peter could see the driver with one hand on the wheel, his phone in the other and watching a movie on another phone, all whilst weaving in and out of the traffic at speeds which far exceeded 150 kilometres per hour. Tucked into the back seat behind the driver I had no such view, and though aware of the suicidal swerving and weaving I was spared the real terror.

There was a moment's respite when we stopped at a roadside tea and coffee stand and the brave front-seat passenger kindly asked if we preferred coffee or tea. I don't remember what we asked for but when he came back to the car juggling five cups in his hands it was quite a surprise when it turned out to be both tea and coffee in the same cup, a novel flavour which lightened things up a bit.

*

In the dim corridors of Baghdad's ancient eighth-century Souq Shorja I had bought an *abaya*[18] specifically for Karbala, where the long black covering is de rigueur for women within the holy precinct. Sparkling feminine ones were pricey so I settled for a plain beanbag style, voluminous, hooded, and with frilly, lacy cuffs adorned with sparkling faux diamonds. It would have been perfect had I been tall and tubby, but I'm neither, and battling to don it I became terribly entangled within its metres of slippery black fabric. The salesman, impressively careful about where he put his hands, came

[18] Long, loose-fitting robe for women, often black, worn over clothes

sleekly to the rescue as Peter dissolved into hysterical giggles, walking away to stem his tears of mirth.

Two days later, dropped on the outskirts of Karbala's sacred perimeter I retreated to the toilets of a random hotel, bound my hair in a white cotton scarf – *hijab*[19] - and donned my *abaya*, emerging looking and feeling every bit a shabby virgin nun. Peter recalls my transformation from a Miss Australia 1975 to a very untidy nun as coinciding with an influx of a large group of Iranian pilgrims and found my sudden appearance into their midst quite spectacular. I wish I could have seen it from his perspective but I was far too busy hitching up my hems and trying to keep a straight face.

With Peter once again dissolving into gurgling hysterics we stumbled out into the streets, and surviving a security check entered the holy precinct and a moving sea of men and women swathed in the ever present black. It was like passing through the looking glass.

Above this scene rose the magnificent blue shrines of Imam Hussein, the Prophet's grandson, and Abbas Ibn Ali, Hussein's half brother, their domes and slender minarets gleaming with gold, walls covered in intricate designs of deep blue and turquoise tiles framed in beige marble. Blue, which symbolises spiritual ascendance. At night the walls glowed from discreet lighting - green, representing fertility and youth, or red for unjustly spilled blood, and swirling around these shrines was the never ending flow of men and women, yes, in black. Black for mourning.

[19] Headscarf, or head-covering, leaving the face visible

If the exteriors are stunning, the shrines' interiors are breathtaking, a celestial glitter of cut-glass and mirror-work in shimmering silver and blues. Las Vegas eat your heart out. A steady hushed hum of moving bodies filled the air, controlled and directed by an army of men and women flourishing great fluffy, brown feather-dusters like magic wands or batons. Coffins of undecorated wood, and a bier with a shrouded body were carried around and around the men's section before exiting to chanted prayer. They would then have been taken to one of Karbala's many cemeteries where to be buried guarantees entrance to paradise.

To get up close to the holy graves of Hussein and Abbas, in each shrine I joined a frenzy of black, bean-bagged women, crushed in like battering rams in a scrum with elbows jabbing and heavy bodies mercilessly pushing, as the feather-dusters swished viciously, blocking and directing the mass of women. Gripping the shrines' metal latticework women wailed, cried tears of anguish, and muttered prayers, while others were silently calm and expressionless. Surrounded by the waves of swirling black and anguished wailing, a heavy and obligatory sadness pervaded, and I wondered just how much of the tearless wailing was forced. But who am I to say.

Essential to grasping the importance of Karbala to the Shia pilgrims is the history of the Sunni-Shia rift. After the Prophet Muhammad died in 632 AD two factions competed for the leadership, and the dispute over the choice of Muhammad's successor would create the

Sunni-Shia split that continues to this day. In short Sunni believed the most respected elder should take over the reins, and the Shia believed leadership should remain within the family. In the years which followed, battles were fought, Muhammad's son-in-law Ali was killed, the Sunni Ummayad dynasty came to power but was rejected by Ali's son Hussein, and in 680 AD the Ummayad caliph sent a large army to confront Hussein at Karbala. With only 72 followers Hussein was hopelessly outnumbered, and all were slaughtered. It is this loss which Shia mourn every year and the memory of which attracts millions of pilgrims to the shrine in Karbala where Hussein's body lies. Seventy-five kilometres away, Najaf too is an equally important place of pilgrimage, for Ali, father of Hussein, is buried there. With the memory of this slaughter kept so vividly alive over the centuries, the schism between Sunni and Shia has never healed.

Covered and carpeted areas outside the shrines offered resting places sheltered from the sun, and were also perfect for absorbing the ambience as endless chanting groups of pilgrims, from Iran, Pakistan, India and beyond circled the shrines. A tall, bearded and turbaned man in biblical dress picked up stray litter, and Pakistani women in colourful clothes and uncontrolled hair were curiously exempt from the wrath of the morality guardians. A boy glided by, holding aloft clouds of dancing, rainbowed balloons, and great rolled carpets were carried from the shrine by an endless army of barefoot men who loaded their cargo onto waiting trucks, bound for the cleaners in what must be a huge and never-ending job.

Despite my determined efforts to conform to the rigid dress rules, I was reprimanded more than once for allowing rebellious wisps of hair to escape my *hijab*. On one occasion, during the fading light of dusk a man approached from behind to alert me to my wayward strands. How had he known? The same evening as we ate falafel sandwiches on the street side we spotted a terrifying guardian lurking outside the shrine. Witch-like, she was wielding a big stick and was clad in a filthy *abaya*. Peter was convinced that she was itching to give me a thwack! Had she found a stray wisp of hair she wouldn't have hesitated. Glimpses of flesh drew attention too, and once a passing woman gently tucked my *abaya* over a sliver of flesh flashing at neck level. A list of do's and don'ts at a security checkpoint advised women that, among other things, they must not laugh. Gales of laughter might have been punished, but smiles were there and fortunately nobody reprimanded me for the more than occasional smothered giggle.

But rules aside, to the essence of this holy place, it was clear that for the pilgrims coming here, this is undoubtedly a highlight of their lives.

Since Hussein's death at the battle of Karbala in the late seventh century, his shrine has been targeted by regular violence, destroyed and rebuilt several times, and with alarming regularity between 2004 and 2010 suffered from bombs and suicide bombers which killed hundreds, wounding many more. In 2019, during

Ashura, the day of mourning Hussein's martyrdom, stampeding pilgrims trampled and killed thirty-one. Given the huge numbers and intense fervour of pilgrims during peak seasons – on just one day in September 2022, 21 million pilgrims came for the Arbaeen commemoration - it is no surprise that iron-fisted organisation and control is necessary and ever present. Battling with a mere one or two hundred women in a scrum was terrifying enough for me.

Despite the impressive crowd control, security checks were cursory, my bag was occasionally halfheartedly prodded or patted but was rarely checked further, and not once did I have to pass through a scanner. Which, looking back, is rather worrying, but hopefully security checks are more thorough during peak mourning periods.

In contrast to Baghdad, Karbala's souqs and streets are pristinely clean, ordered, and cheerful, overhung by colourful lighting in the shapes of butterflies and flowers which hovered, purple and yellow, above the night-time streets and lanes. Surrounded by luggage and shopping bags, sour-faced old crones perched cross-legged on flat carts as they were pushed through the crowds by young men and boys, and along the busy, covered Jumhurya Street I stopped to taste a small portion of a divine looking sweet, all cream and caramel. It was delicious, and once again my payment was refused. The kindness of the Iraqis still humbles me. Further along the street a line of glass cabinets stocked with foreign currency notes and Iraqi dinar belonged to money-changers who were often astonishingly absent. Where else in the world would someone leave an open cabinet chock-a-block with money unattended? But security clearly has different priorities, for on the same street I was threatened with arrest when casually, and foolishly, photographing a fire truck which was parked inaccessibly behind a line of busy pavement stalls. I was only thinking that in an emergency the stallholders and goods would have been flattened. Very naive of me.

As a pilgrim city, Karbala is awash with hotels, ranging from glitzy to seedy, and tempted by a special deal we chose the glitzy glass and marble Gulf Tower Hotel, with its cavernous lobby and a glass-bubble lift rising through five floors. Here we met a man who had long ago lost a leg during the war with Iran, but he told us the story as a matter of fact, without complaint. It was an utterly moving and humbling moment. By night an invisible male singer serenaded a newly married couple and in the process all the other hotel residents as his voice rose through the cathedral-like lobby in a heavenly performance which lasted hours. And over breakfast we met a charming, young Australian-Afghan man with his mother, who looked like his older sister. They were all smiles as they told us they were on their way to Iran to see his wife. I didn't ask if this would be the first meeting, or if his wife had a visa for Australia, but I wished him luck. Elsewhere a friend staying in a cheaper hotel had a room with attached bathroom, and a toilet jammed into such a tight space that he had to perform yogic acrobatics to use it. He also spent much time pondering the clothes hooks which were attached upside down to the wall, and never quite understood the logic of the management's mathematics either, as when leaving he paid significantly less than expected, despite his attempts to pay the correct and higher price. We too were undercharged – either the Karbalites are working to a different mathematical logic, or it simply isn't their forte. But this is Iraq.

In need of a day's break from the intensity of Karbala we caught a minibus from the intriguingly named Karbala Unified Garage to Najaf, where Imam Ali, the Prophet's cousin and son-in-law, is buried in a shrine of cream bricks decorated with gorgeous, delicate patterns in shades of blue and with the usual cut-glass interior extravaganza. Stunning. Oddly, an officious young female security guard took offence at the sight of my socked feet. Speechless, she glared at them, clearly horrified, before pointing aggressively to the exit, and shouting 'OUT!' No amount of questioning hand-flapping by me would change her mind, and I never discovered what offended her, for the same socks had been acceptable in Karbala shrines. But by this time, beginning to overdose on the glitter, I was content to gaze at the heavenly exteriors and endless parade of assorted pilgrims instead. I also, however, discovered with joyful revenge another entrance to the women's section, where my socks posed no threat to the shimmering interior.

Peter's experience was so very different to mine and in his words he captures the overwhelming soul of the shrines - *'One of my lingering memories of our visits to the shrines took place in Najaf. Amid the feather duster wielding guardians, the clamour around the tombs, the fabulousity of the shrines themselves, I came across an elderly man, alone, sitting gazing in silence at the tomb with wordless tears streaming down his cheeks. It was moving and particularly so as he was grieving for someone who had died centuries ago. His grief was still raw and seemed more genuine than any other I had seen that day…'*

Peter saw many more coffins being paraded through the men's section of the mosque than I did, and no doubt, after leaving Ali's shrine the coffins were bound for Najaf's Wadi-al-Salaam - Valley of Peace - cemetery, the largest in the world. The final resting place of six million bodies, and covering almost 1,500 acres, it too attracts millions of pilgrims every year. We passed it on our way back to the main road and peeked in through small arched entrances, looking at the crowded graves, many of them smooth mud mounds blending beautifully with the surroundings. But the size of it was too overwhelming and we didn't go in.

*

On the Euphrates ten kilometres from Najaf is Kufa, first capital of the Abbasid Caliphate, and the second settlement ever planned and built by Muslims as they advanced beyond Arabia. In its heyday, between the eighth and tenth centuries, it was a thriving centre for intellectuals and lends its name to the Kufic script, more angular and rigid than later and more flamboyant scripts. I'm ashamed to admit that I had never heard of

Kufa and knew none of this when I visited, but with no expectations it was all the more thrilling to find that Kufa was the highlight of the day.

Signposted as '*The Great Mosque of Cough*' [sic], Kufa's seventh-century mosque is one of the oldest and holiest surviving mosques in the world, and in contrast to the extravagance of Najaf and Karbala's shrines, its exterior walls offer a sober beauty in unadorned cream bricks which only emphasise the rich blue, white and yellow tile-work of the main arched entrance and its adjacent old minaret.

Passing through the first entrance we emerged into a wide space between wall and mosque, and into a party atmosphere in full swing, with free food being distributed and a far more relaxed ambience than Najaf or Karbala. People were actually having fun, and showing it. I was almost shocked to see some young men smoking, and instead of lambasting me for my socks a security guard asked where I was from and if I would marry him as he blew me a kiss.

Inside the mosque, a grand white marble courtyard is surrounded by carpeted halls with wooden ceilings supported on marching rows of white marble columns, a design said to have developed from the floor plan of the Prophet Muhammad's house. Some halls shimmer with cut-glass and beautiful decorative tile work, but on a more subdued scale than in Najaf and Karbala.

As Peter chatted to a gentle Ayatollah from Bamiyan, Afghanistan, I was ushered into men-only areas by guardians keen to show me the tombs. It was an open-minded delight, and so refreshing after the tight-laced guardians of the other shrines. The masses of pilgrims at Karbala and Najaf were happily absent, so we lingered, absorbing the overwhelming peace and calm, and would have stayed longer had we not wanted to be back in Karbala before dark. Walking back to the main road we left behind the spiritual serenity and were plunged back into the modern world. As we passed a clothes shop with a spectacular, bright orange jacket on display, it flashed through my mind that this was a jacket which Michael Portillo would not resist.

The airy Great Mosque of Kufa

Not long after leaving Najaf on a crammed minibus, a passenger asked the driver to stop by a stall selling small, colourful plaster statues of panthers, playful kittens, and ducks. He returned ten minutes later, not with a plaster kitten, but with bottles of water which he distributed to everyone aboard. Grumbled mutterings indicated that not everyone was pleased at the delay, but apparently this was a special day on the religious calendar, and such offerings were part of religious duty.

Making up for lost time our over-confident young driver continued along the highway in wild F1 fashion, passing two grisly car accidents in quick succession, one apparently quite fresh, and seeing a body amongst the wreckage Peter thoughtfully advised me not to look. You'd think such carnage would sober the driver, but he flew on at lunatic speed, zigzagging in and out between slower cars as terrified, I gripped the seat in front of me. Closer to Karbala we saw an SUV driving confidently straight into oncoming traffic, a sight which became all too normal on Iraqi roads. All I can say is 'This is Iraq.'

*

We left Karbala the following day on a GMC from the Karbala Unified Garage, and walking there through side streets to avoid security checks I tripped on the trailing hems of my oversized *abaya* and tumbled to the ground in a cloud of billowing black and a fit of giggles. Despite the occasional grumbles, I confess that being wrapped and bound in black was an extraordinary learning experience, living for a short time the daily reality of millions of women in this world.

Taking it upon himself to maintain my image of respectability, Peter had borrowed a silver clothes peg from a scarf shop, clipping the wayward *abaya* closed where it gaped lewdly open at my neckline, but my hems continued to trail through the dust. Tripping and stumbling in and out of minibuses, I began to master the art of delicately hitching up the trailing fabric while manoeuvring steps and stairs and unexpectedly began to enjoy its sensual swirling and swaying as I moved. Interestingly, when I was finally free to hesitantly disrobe I felt oddly exposed, despite the relief at leaving behind my short-lived life as a pious black beanbag.

Reluctant to leave my faithful friend, the *abaya* accompanied me, stuffed into a plastic bag, down to Basrah and back to Baghdad, 'just in case', before coming to an ignominious demise when I sadly abandoned it on a chair in my hotel room. By this time it had lost its faux diamonds which had been glued on, and was decidedly grubby, but at times I wish I had kept it, just for the memory of the many hours of happy entertainment it offered. I still have the silver butterfly clip though.

***

Woman on cart, Jumhurya Street

Wall panel inside the Kufa Mosque

Top: Babylon's mythical Mushussu
Bottom: Aurochs and mushussu marching across Babylon's ancient walls

4

BABYLON

Babylon. Ancient, fabled city of Mesopotamia on the Lower Euphrates.

Dating back almost 4,000 years, from its beginnings as a minor state in 1894 BC to its eventual demise in 549 BC, the history of Babylon is littered with the names of passing dynasties and a long list of kings and conquerors. Hammurabi, who ruled from around 1792–1750 BC, turned Babylon into a major power, and Nebuchadnezzar II, who ruled for 49 years until his death in 562 BC, was the longest reigning and greatest of the kings, remembered today for his building projects and beautification of Babylon, including the construction and restoration of temples, palaces, the Ishtar gate, and the Processional Way. Some believe he built the Hanging Gardens of Babylon, but others dispute this, believing the Gardens are in Nineveh. He was also famous for his military campaigns in the Levant and the destruction of Jerusalem in 586 BC. But Nebuchadnezzar was not just about beautification and destruction, he also built canals to bring water from the Euphrates and began work on the Royal Canal, completed under King Nabonidus, linking the Euphrates to the Tigris, an ambitious project which transformed agriculture in the region. Alas, it seems to have vanished. Much of what we see now in the ancient city's ruins dates from Nebuchadnezzar's rule.

Only 50 kilometres south-east of Karbala it's easy to visit Babylon in a day, so after breakfasting on *zataar*[20] rolls and pretzels we boarded a minibus at 9.00 AM, bound for Hillah, the closest town to Babylon's ancient ruins. We were looking forward to a refreshing day out escaping the hustle and bustle of Iraqi cities. From Hillah we had trouble finding a taxi driver who understood the name Babylon and every variation we could think of, and it was only when I recalled the Arabic word for ruins – *athaar* – that we finally found a taxi driver who understood. But even he got lost along the way. Twenty minutes later, after driving out of Hillah and through a shrubby expanse of wasteland, we came to a small cream brick building where we bought our tickets, or rather paid our money, as we never received a paper ticket, and continued down a long stretch of road at the end of which gleamed the unmissable blue of the Ishtar Gate.

The Ishtar Gate is probably the best known symbol of Babylon. What we see today is a replica of the original which is in the Pergamon Museum, Berlin, but no

[20] Zataar is a blend of thyme, oregano, sesame seeds and other herbs, used in Middle Eastern cuisine

matter, it is still striking. Once at the starting point of the Processional Way it must have dazzled and awed the Mesopotamian people and visiting dignitaries with its glazed brickwork shimmering in a deep blue, the colour of lapis lazuli, with sacred *aurochs*, and *mushussu*[21] depicted in shades of gold, yellow and white bas-relief brickwork. Below these sacred animals was a glazed frieze of white and yellow chamomile flowers on a black background. The animals symbolised the gods Marduk (*mushussu*), and Adad (*aurochs*) and guarded the entrances to Mesopotamian temples and palaces. The chamomile flowers symbolised Ishtar, goddess of fertility and victory in war.

We'd been told that a guide would meet us at the entrance, but with no sign of him we wandered off alone until we were stopped and told we must join a small group of Romanian ladies. 'Why?' we asked. To prevent people from pillaging, which made sense. Iraq takes the theft of ancient treasures seriously and we had recently read of a British geologist sentenced to fifteen years in prison for attempting to smuggle shards out of the country. Shards. His sentence was later overturned, but nonetheless….

And so we entered the inner zones of old Babylon, shadowing the Processional Way where the remains of original paving glued in place by black bitumen were still clearly visible. It's a long, wide, straight strip, now flanked by occasional trees on one side and the old city

---

[21] Aurochs – bull of an extinct species of cattle; mushussu - a mythical long-necked dragon

walls on the other. Further on, the guide unlocked a padlocked gate and we trod gently down a flight of stairs leading to a sunken section of the road lined with high, beige brick walls. Rising above us, depicted on the brickwork were many more bulls and *mushussu*, marching along the walls on both sides of the street, unglazed, the same colour as the rest of the brickwork, and still striking. These were original, not recreations, their muscular bodies capturing the subtleties of movement and depicted with exquisitely fine detail. As we all gazed upwards, utterly transfixed by their repeated images moving across the walls, a reverent hush descended. Across the millennia these sacred creatures were still exerting the same power they had held over all who walked this way thousands of years ago. Totally speechless, for a short time we were lost, humbled in the moment.

The spell was broken as the guard ushered us out and onward to visit a temple where the original walls were being restored with bricks made of mud and straw, using the same technique the Mesopotamians had used so long ago. Beyond that, past a honeycomb cluster of partially excavated ruins we came to more walls, ancient, not restored, where, if you looked carefully, you could find an occasional brick embedded with cuneiform writing, recording the name of Nebuchadnezzar II and dates of construction. Beyond that, in newer walls, were similar bricks embedded with Arabic writing recording Saddam Hussein's contribution to the restoration of Babylon's walls in the 1980s.

Recording your name for posterity is nothing new, leaders are still doing just that, whether it be in written form, or the construction and naming of a museum, stadium, airport, university or city… the list goes on. Many have criticised Saddam for portraying himself as a latter day Nebuchadnezzar, but in the end it all comes down to the same thing. Kings, leaders, dictators, presidents and prime ministers, they all want to be remembered for a good deed, a public construction, a highway… nothing has changed.

I had thought that much of Babylon had been destroyed over the years, especially after 2003 when the US and Polish military occupied the site causing much damage, so I was thrilled to find there are still large areas of surviving though crumbling walls and foundations. In order to recreate the grandeur of the South Palace, Saddam rebuilt the high walls on the original foundations and has been much criticised for the clumsy and often damaging techniques and materials used. Whether it is an accurate reconstruction or not, it does give an inkling of the size and splendour of the royal courts or halls, which would have been magnificent. Our guide pointed out how, for security reasons, doorways between the series of interlinking halls were positioned so that there was no clear view between the first and the last. And a little further on, off to one side, is a huge maze of zigzagging corridors and rooms in geometrical perfection, built to confuse invaders. Security has always been an issue.

In the small museum we finally met the man who should have been our guide. He'd grown up on the site following in the tracks of his father before him, and spoke of his arrest by the US military when he had confronted them stealing artefacts. Thrown into prison he had his arms and ribs broken and spent a month in a windowless cell without seeing the light of day. He had a gentle, almost innocent face which betrayed none of the horror he must have experienced, and not for the first time I asked myself, how is that possible?

In the late 1980s Saddam had a nearby local village destroyed. In its place rose an artificial man-made hill, and there, high up and overlooking the ruins of ancient Babylon, Saddam built a summer palace with sweeping views over his 'kingdom'. Seen from the ruins below its presence looms intimidatingly fortress-like in the near distance, and drawn by this hovering vision we followed a road leading up to it, walking through the cool, shady greenery of parkland as loud, joyful music bounced through the trees. People were coming here to relax and enjoy, there was gaiety in the air, and in front of a small cafe a statue of a deranged wizard-like character inexplicably bore a tray offering paper roses in red, purple and white. We walked on past manicured gardens which line the road as it spirals around the mound and upwards to the palace entrance. From the top the views are spectacular, the extent and shapes of the ruins become clearer, and date plantations seem to go on forever in a sea of greenery on either side of the Euphrates as it flows gently by.

And then of course there is the palace, multi-storeyed, faced with honey coloured stone, massive and semi-fortress-like, it speaks of power. Its high doorways were open, and oddly, not a guard or a gun was in sight. Stepping cautiously through the main entrance we entered a hall of hushed stillness, its walls decorated with stylised date palms, and murmuring doves and smaller birds nesting in the chandeliers, too high to be vandalised. We passed through room after room where vandals and looters have left their mark after Saddam's downfall - graffiti was sprayed and daubed on walls, but instead of anti-Saddam slogans it appeared to be mostly declarations of love written in great swirls of black and blue Arabic. Arabic is a beautiful, sensual script but here it seemed offensive, sullying the once pristine walls. A grand staircase leading to the darkened upper floors was blocked by rolls of razor-wire and great logs of wood, a lift, its broken doors prised half open was frozen in time, and windows had been smashed. Broken glass and tiles littered the floors. But behind the vandalism were lingering traces of finery in the carved wooden panels and inlaid work on ceilings, the details of sophisticated light fittings, the Arabic designs in tile-work. Ignoring the occasional frescoes of Saddam celebrating his military power, there was still a certain elegance, highlighted by the eerie emptiness of the palace. Outside a large, empty swimming pool was home to broken tiles and windblown rubbish, and added to the sense of abandonment. I can understand the destruction and vandalism, but it still saddened me to see it, as this had been, despite everything, a beautiful place. What remains is a haunting beauty intertwined with tragedy.

On the exterior walls, above the doors, profiles of Saddam's head were incorporated into military insignia and symbols of ancient Mesopotamia. But then that's not unusual. From ancient times to the modern day, emperors, kings and dictators alike have stamped their profiles on coins, bank notes and buildings. Nothing new in that. Whether we approve or not, it is history nonetheless. Interestingly, after the rabid anti-Saddam frenzy of twenty years ago, views have already begun to change and now photos of Saddam grace busses and shop windows in neighbouring Jordan where he has been resurrected as a hero for many.

There is talk of converting Saddam's many palaces into museums, and perhaps some day this palace will house Babylon's treasures. It could make a marvellous hotel too, and I can easily imagine sitting out on a wide balcony or terrace enjoying the sweeping views overlooking the date plantations, the Euphrates reflecting a blue sky, and the ancient walls of Babylon still standing as a reminder of what had once been.

We left reluctantly, and stopped to snack on the remnants of our lunch by the side of the road. Looking back up at the palace, its stone mass rising high above us, I recognised in the inward slanting walls a tribute to the design of ancient ziggurats. The building was designed to awe, to intimidate perhaps, but in that moment I could only see a nod to the past. And I liked it. On the hillside below a young couple were enjoying the modern version of the Garden of Eden. There was a sweetness and innocence in the air which wouldn't have been there thirty years go. Babylon is many things, and it still has magic.

***

Top: Saddam's Palace overlooking the ruins of Babylon
Bottom: Graffitied walls inside Saddam's Palace

Top: Ziggurat of Ur, looming large
Bottom: Stairway to the gods, Ziggurat of Ur

5

NASIRIYAH
THE ZIGGURAT OF UR
and
THE MARSHES

Nasiriyah straddles the Euphrates in southern Iraq and is young by Iraqi standards. The town itself has nothing of ancient splendour to offer tourists - no grand mosques, madrasahs, or crumbling fortified walls, but the great Ziggurat of Ur is only twenty kilometres southwest of the city, and the marshes where Wilfred Thesiger[22] spent long periods of time back in the 1950s, are just under ninety kilometres to the east.

Three of us, Peter, myself and Nick, who we'd found sprawling in the back seats of a minibus at the Karbala Unified Garage, had arrived after a four-hour drive down the usual long, straight desert highway, with a pause at one of those typical roadside feeding areas with great cavernous dining halls big enough to welcome a

---

[22] British explorer best known for his books on travels in Arabia and Iraq during the mid-20th century

wedding party, or two, if need be. As other passengers dined in a civilised manner on kebabs and roast chicken, we perused the snacks on offer in the window of a small shop, and watched in delight as a small mouse, oblivious to his audience, brazenly nibbled on assorted packets of nuts and biscuits. He was having a wonderful time.

From there the road continued south through a desert now punctuated with splashes of swamp and occasional camels, cows and sheep. It was good to see the presence of animal life again, and it was also exciting to cross the fabled Euphrates.

Many would describe Nasiriyah as nondescript, and true, the town's outskirts are blandly unimpressive, but as the traffic crawled towards the town centre, passing a market where vegetables and fresh fish were spread on grubby sackcloth by the roadside, there was the promise of more down-to-earth and colourful things to come. We were dropped in the centre at a roundabout close to the Hotel Hammurabi, and our delightful driver, thrilled to have foreigners aboard, in true Iraqi style invited us for lunch - an offer we politely refused.

At the top of a staircase lined with fake green grass, the Hammurabi was simple and basic, beds came with one sheet only, but our room was clean, and had its own bathroom complete with a portable toilet seat for geriatrics over a squat toilet. It also sported a TurboCooler which spewed cold air into the room with a racket akin to the roaring blades of a helicopter.

Less happy with the grimy single room on offer, Nick checked into a windowless room at the ZamZam Hotel just down the road, managed by Mr. Chuckles, the grumpy manager whose hair was either plastered to his head with thick layers of gel, or he was wearing a plastic wig. Mr Chuckles had a habit of hunkering down behind the reception counter and vanishing in the blink of an eye. We suspected he was a *djinn*[23], and had perhaps transformed into the cockroach scuttling towards the reception area couch. He spoke very little English but communicated with grunts, or if necessary a flapping sign language only he truly understood.

On one occasion, attempting to pay Chuckles for an extra night, Nick waved cash in front of him through clouds of cigarette smoke. Chuckles refused. So Nick retreated to his room and was just settling down when Chuckles and his henchman hammered on the door demanding the money. Chuckles' unpredictable behaviour and incessant grumpiness became a regular source of great amusement to us - things were looking good on the entertainment front in Nasiriyah.

We stayed four days and I became very fond of the town and her people who were astonishingly friendly and curious. We tramped the banks of the Euphrates, following a rutted track of dusty, dried mud which in better days could have been a pleasant, meandering garden walk, we passed dank buildings, former clubs and cafes now blackened by fire and splattered with

[23] In Arabic/Muslim mythology, a spirit in human or animal form, able to possess humans

bullet holes, and we sat awhile on a sticky bench overlooking the river, watching fishermen casting lines and small boats floating tranquilly on the current. In a smart cafe overlooking the Euphrates groups of young men sat cross-legged in red-rugged niches feasting on mysterious dishes while we nibbled on chicken sandwiches washed down with the restaurant's speciality, True Gastro Ayran Drink.

In the afternoons we sipped tea in an open-fronted tea shop opposite the Hammurabi, sitting on carpeted benches inside, or at tables which spilled out onto the roadside, offering the added excitement of being in the midst of dodgem car chaos. A number of oddball, glazed-eyed men frequented it, and Nick dubbed it the Day Release Cafe. One young man who spoke excellent English offered to help us get tickets for the Ziggurat, kindly phoning us later to see if we had been successful, and on another occasion we shared a table with a man who had lost both legs during the last war. Courtesy of the US, he now lived in Wisconsin. He generously invited us for tea and snacks, but his constant talk of money, money, money wore a little thin and escape became necessary. As dusk set in one evening we paused on a bridge to gaze down on a small outdoor cafe, its tables and chairs erratically sloping down the dusty riverbank. A young man sat alone, reading, and by the light of small lamps it looked almost romantic.

Nasiriyah's souq burst into life in the evenings, vibrant with colour, bright flashing lights and assorted goods. We installed ourselves in an excellent fruit juice shop where we sat on colourful plastic chairs surrounded by a bevy of buxom, heavily made-up young women who shyly mustered the courage to practise their English, especially on Peter and Nick. They were delighted and delightful, full of smiles and giggles, and any lulls in the chatting were filled by a television cartoon chirpily teaching children Arabic.

In search of a place to play backgammon, we were tempted by a pleasantly seedy cafe in a side street, where in the evening young men clustered around dimly lit tables overhung by leafy trees, and we settled into comfortable couches inside, amongst the smoke and perfume of water pipes and a buzz of noise from the television. Intent on playing *tawla* we attracted a group of bright eyed, snappily dressed young men who cheerily told us we played badly and promptly ambushed the game. One of them, a young lawyer, insisted on playing Peter while I was left, like a fairy grandmother surrounded by the rest of the gang, to answer questions ranging from world politics to learning English. Seeing that I was struggling to keep my wayward head scarf in place, they declared that 'the hijab is not obligatory', insisting that it is 'freedom of choice', and I loved them for that. We went there several times, and each time we met the same young men, who grilled us with questions and advised us on how to play backgammon, and each time it was impossible to pay for our tea. I was always the only woman in the cafe, and as usual, I was treated with enormous respect. There seemed to be an obvious gay gathering there as well.

Many of the lads sported a very sultry hairstyle - the Nasiriyah style - longer on one side and draped seductively over one eye, occasionally sensually flicked back with a feminine pout. Add a certain way of moving and it was clear there was something going on. And this in a small town where I'd have expected a much more conservative population. But surprises lay around every corner in Nasiriyah. That first evening, as we left the cafe we were serenaded and applauded by the outside *shebab*. We felt like royalty.

*

We'd come to Nasiriyah specifically to see the Ziggurat of Ur. In fact it was *the* reason I'd come to Iraq.

Ziggurat - from *ziqqurratum* in ancient Assyrian, meaning height or pinnacle.

Part of a temple complex, a ziggurat is a step pyramid, consisting of two to seven layers, walls angling inwards as they rise to a platform where a temple honouring the patron god of the city would have stood. As dwelling places for the gods Mesopotamian ziggurats were not for public worship and only priests were given access. Made of a solid mass of mud bricks, 64 metres long and 45 metres wide, the Ziggurat of Ur rises in three levels faced with burnt bricks welded together by bitumen. Built around 2100 BC by the Sumerian king Ur-Nammu, the Ziggurat of Ur is one of only twenty-five surviving ziggurats, mostly found in Iraq and scattered through the ancient lands of Sumer, Babylonia, and Assyria.

Along the way we'd heard mixed reports about the Ziggurat - some foreigners had been refused entrance, others had no problem, but the fact is that in Iraq you never know. Checkpoints are manned by different militias, and everything is very much according to the whim of whoever is manning a checkpoint on any particular day. You just have to go and see.

On arrival in Nasiriyah we wasted no time dashing to the museum where, and only there, tickets for the Ziggurat must be purchased in advance. We had heard it was not possible to buy tickets at the Ziggurat. Alas it was a Friday, the weekend, and when we rolled up at the museum entrance the gates were firmly closed. Closed until Sunday. We were more than crestfallen. A resident guard advised us to go to the Ziggurat, assuring us we'd be able to get tickets there, but was he fobbing us off? Was it true? With no choice and with our hopes dashed, we aborted efforts to find another solution and left, the spring in our steps now gone. Two pretty young women cheered us up a little as they stopped to practise their English, though our hopes for success with the tickets remained low. But there were worse things in the world and watching the Euphrates flowing by drew us back to the present, and the magic of the moment.

The next morning, Saturday, we negotiated with a taxi to take us to the Ziggurat, and off we went, bright and early, into the unknown distance to see what fate held in store for us. Nerves aflutter as we arrived at the checkpoint, we were taken into a small security hut and told to sit and wait. Which we did, sitting stiffly upright, very much like naughty schoolkids expecting the worst in a headmaster's office. Unsmiling, the officer took his time, exercising his power by flicking slowly through each of our passports, perusing every page as we waited in fearful doubt, squirming with the mounting, agonising tension. After a very long moment he flicked through the passports once again, this time pausing to photograph necessary pages. Yet another tense pause followed before he leaned forward and solemnly handed our passports back. With a sudden smile he asked for the 25,000 dinar entrance fee.

We were ecstatic, and treasured tickets in hands, once outside we literally danced and jumped with an uncontrolled joy I shall never forget.

Three happy travellers – Peter, the author, and Nick

Nor shall I forget the presence of the Ziggurat, which, at first just a small blot on the horizon, grew larger and larger as we approached until it stood before us, magnificent, grand and proud, silently speaking of its ancient past. A past spanning four thousand years. True, it has been restored several times over the millennia - in the sixth century BC by King Nabonidus, and again, partially, in the 1980s by Saddam Hussein who restored the facade and monumental staircase - but even partly in ruin its massive presence continues to awe.

It towered over us, its solid mass rising 30 metres from the sands, its sheer walls, punctuated with 'weeper-holes' for drainage, narrowing slightly inwards as they rose through three levels. A monumental staircase led steeply, directly upwards to the top, now a flat, crumbled expanse of scattered bricks. Other smaller staircases gave access to the different levels, some descending to nowhere and ending in a sudden drop.

Climbing to the top, now an empty space where once a temple to the moon god Nanna would have stood, we looked out at an infinite sea of sand in all directions as our feet scuffed against a litter of ancient mud bricks, some still welded together in clumps by the original black bitumen. It was like looking out at eternity.

Standing alone, isolated in that endless expanse of sand the Ziggurat is overwhelmingly stunning. It is also a reminder of grandeur fallen. Think of Shelley's poem, Ozymandias. But the memory of grandeur remains nonetheless, and continues.

As I gazed and absorbed the presence of this mighty survivor from the ancient past, I wondered at the vision and enormous work needed to create such a massive structure. How many of our modern buildings will last four thousand years? We may have the technology and sophisticated equipment to create higher and higher towers and shapes which defy safety, but they won't last. The glass will shatter, wind, dust, seeds and rain will enter. Birds, lizards and ants will do their work, the buildings will crumble. A skeletal scaffolding of ugly reinforced concrete might remain. But little more.

Not far from the mighty Ziggurat were other ruins amongst the sand, still under excavation. A sign described the site as the 'holy sanitary' [sic], and informed us that it included 'huge wells' and 'many facilities and rooms'. A security guard told me it was the Royal Palace.

Still further on again was another excavation site, fenced off, and without any information boards. I imagine this included the so-called 'Great Death Pit', part of the Royal Tombs, where 1,800 bodies were discovered in the 1920s, along with pots, gold jewellery set with precious stones, and the so-called Standard of Ur, a medium-sized inlaid box of unknown purpose depicting scenes from war, people making offerings, and a banquet, and the 45.7cm high Ram in a Thicket statue, whose horns suggest it is more likely a goat, covered with precious metals and stones. The two pieces indicate the high level of sophistication of the Ur civilisation. At the time I'd never heard of Ur's treasures and wouldn't discover them until several months later when I visited the British Museum in London. One word can describe them: exquisite.

Walking through the dusty remains of the Palace area I had no idea just how rich and sophisticated the city of Ur had been, but it had clearly been breathtaking.

Knowing nothing of the Ziggurat's treasures, for two hours we were transfixed solely by the size, magnificence and aura of the structure. Surveying the desert from the top, I thought I could detect lines and markings in the sand surrounding the site. Were they the last traces of the once great city of Ur?

*

Flying High on the Ziggurat

***

Early morning the following day, we were bound for Chibayish on a minibus driven by a gentle giant with enormous hands. He was a careful driver, and the bus's windscreen was one of the few in Iraq which was not badly cracked. In Chibayish we were dropped on the main road in front of a lone restaurant at a T-intersection, a semi-desolate place with little sign of a bustling town, though later I would see an aerial photograph which shows the town sprawling along the banks of a waterway, much larger than it seemed at the ground-level intersection. As though expecting us, we were met by a man claiming to belong to tourist security, and with little choice we allowed him to lead us to a waterway where several long, narrow Marsh boats were moored, some with their outboard motors wrapped in colourful tea cosy-like coverings. A *mudhif*, the traditional reed house of the Marsh Arabs stood nearby, its structure entirely made of tied bundles of reed, standing straight as soldiers at the *mudhif's* entrance, arching in great curved beams supporting the roof of woven reed matting, and filtering the light and air through latticed reed walls and windows. The floor was covered with a blue and white mat, and a solitary light bulb hung from one of the reed beams. The *mudhif* might have been there for tourists but it was a gorgeous work of art, made with nothing but reeds.

Reed construction

Inside a Mudhif

Abbas, a handsome and softly spoken young boatman with an explosive Baghdadi hairstyle, rather like a chef's *toque*[24], took us on a chugging two-hour trip through time and magic as he manoeuvred his long, narrow boat

---

[24] Tall white hat worn by chefs

slowly through waterways lined with tall, swaying feathery reeds, and alive with birds - dozens of black and white kingfishers, egrets, the occasional falcon, and more. Tall, willowy and statuesque fishermen clad in long robes stood silently punting their boats through the water in the traditional way and fishing with nets. Every movement was graceful. Water buffalo, their leathery skin shining black in the water came into view, swimming slowly or wallowing amongst the reeds, casting languid looks our way.

Mudhifs in the marshes

At a muddy embankment cluttered with shabby reed and wire enclosures we stopped to visit some of Abbas's seven boisterous brothers who were guarding their buffaloes. We stayed awhile with them under their shelter, little more than a sagging roof of reed matting. Basic, muddy and smelly, it was a far cry from a refined *mudhif*, but it was real. Removing our shoes we sat cross-legged on grubby rugs covering the damp ground though they thoughtfully offered an upturned bucket topped with a cushion to sit on, as they cheekily asked us our age, whether we were married, and if not, why not? Leaving them as they dissolved into childish giggles, we clambered back onto our colourful cushions in the narrow boat and puttered back through small waterways, past the remains of a bridge Saddam had built, and finally stopped at a shining silver dome which rose from the marshes. Not a mosque as I had originally thought, but the Martyrs Monument, in memory of the Marsh Arabs slaughtered by Saddam Hussein after the 1991 Gulf War. Tragic and sobering, photos of the graves and faces of those who were killed or simply vanished lined the silent space inside the monument. It was hauntingly moving.

Before returning to Nasiriyah we lunched on tender kebabs in the solitary, and modern restaurant on the main road, and were befriended by a local man who now lives in Western Australia. He was delighted to meet us and especially to make an Aussie connection, and as he left he called across to us that he had paid for our meals. NO! NO! NO! we cried in unison, but too late. This is Iraq.

Draining of the marshes for agriculture and oil exploration began as far back as the 1950s, and, furthered by Saddam Hussein in the years following 1991, the marshes were reduced to a horrifying 10% of their original size and the population decimated. But with the waters flowing again after 2003 the population rebounded, only to be confronted now by falling water levels due to drought and the damming of the water sources in Turkey. It was evident as we drove back to Nasiriyah, past swathes of parched, cracked earth and a landscape brown with dead reeds, that the damage to the Marshes is huge. An old Marsh Arab with us in the taxi muttered and shook his head as he pointed to the wasteland. We didn't need to speak Arabic to understand.

***

Gathering reeds in the marshes

Top: Buffalo and shelter in the marshes
Bottom: 'Tea cosy' engines

Ceiling in old house, Basrah

6

BASRAH

I knew little of Basrah, only that centuries ago Sindbad sailed from there, bound for adventures in faraway exotic places. I knew it was once a proud city of fine homes with gorgeously carved wooden *shanasheel* latticework. I also knew that following the 2003 invasion it was bombarded with depleted uranium munitions, coating the city with lethal dust along with particles of lead and mercury from other weapons, resulting in an explosion of cancer and birth deformities. I knew too that it is an oil rich city.

The road to Basrah is long and straight, crossing a desert devoid of vegetation but laced with fiery flares and black smoke from nearby oil fields. Smoke which contains cancer causing pollutants. Fifty kilometres west of Basrah, Rumaila is the largest of the oil fields, and considering the high rate of leukemia among residents of North Rumaila and a 20% rise in cancer in Basrah between 2015 and 2018, it doesn't take much to connect the dots. The Iraqi government owns these oil fields, but the lead contractors include BP and the Italian company Eni. 'Murky' is a word which comes to mind.

The highway and spaghetti junctions leading into the sprawling city are clogged with afternoon traffic jams, and on the surface, Basrah is modern, wealthy and stocked with the same consumer goods found in any western city. A newly paved Corniche runs beside the wide waters of the Shatt al-Arab, refreshing the eyes and lungs after the dusty desert. It's a haven for young and old, to meet, stroll, run, and cycle in the cool evening air. Young women dip toes in the river and pose for selfies, while men and boys fish. A dancing fountain erupts at dusk to the jaunty beat of Arab pop music, and one of Saddam Hussein's pleasure boats is still moored nearby. Oddly, it is still afloat and looks surprisingly undamaged, while long abandoned casino and party boats are half sinking in the satin waters of the Shatt. Homeless people have moved into some of them, and teenage lads dive from pontoon jetties, swimming back to the banks where the occasional rat scurries.

But behind the modern facade are parts of Basrah's heritage where streets are overhung by monstrous webs of tangled wiring, old houses with *shanasheel* windows are collapsing from neglect, and a network of old canals, once clean enough to drink from, are now choked with rubbish. Living here in collapsing buildings, with the stench of putrid open drains is not for the wealthy, and it was no surprise to learn the old houses are inhabited mostly by squatters. But restoration is afoot, selected old buildings are being given a new life, one of them the former Sheikh Khazaal Mansion, now a cultural centre. We were welcomed inside for a peek at the major restoration project in progress and met three delightful young women, all apprentice engineers, working there. The spacious home, overlooking a canal, had been magnificent. Full of refined details, one of which was a frieze of chamomile flowers edging the gallery surrounding the inner courtyard.... flowers reminiscent of Babylon. Outside another team was valiantly rebuilding the sagging walls of the canal, a filthy and frustrating job battling the accumulated rubbish clogging the waters. We chatted to the chief engineer who offered us tea and his strikingly sturdy business card, should we ever need his drainage services.

*

Sheikh Khazaal Mansion restoration in progress

Top: Shanasheel houses, catching the breeze
Bottom: Doorway in old Basrah

*

Less than ten minutes walk from the Shatt al-Arab, on Istiklal Street we stayed in the Al Buraq Hotel, an erratically lopsided structure reminiscent of collapsing buildings in Baghdad. But it was not collapsing. No, its crazy angles were designed to create visual havoc, and it certainly had personality. An intriguing notice recommended *'the use of rail funds, Deposit box and widgets value because the administration is not responsible for any loses'* [sic], and continuing the erratic lines of the exterior facade, our room had no right angles. It also had a mysterious dwarf door to nowhere, a bathroom with two toilets, western and squat, a sloping shower stall which was terrifyingly slippery when wet, and rusty water spurting from the hot tap, as I discovered when washing my white scarf. It was a busy hotel and we appeared to be the only western foreigners. I only ever saw Arab guests in the lobby, mostly businessmen, though one evening two buxom, heavily made-up women in black *abayas* aglitter with bling made an appearance, staring at us in brazen interest. We were not quite sure if they were indeed women, or otherwise.

Just down the road from the hotel was a shop selling bathroom ware, offering a display of ultra-bling, gilded, yes gilded, squat toilets, with basins to match. Just as stunning as the loos themselves, was the fact that they were permanently outside on the pavement, night and day, even when the shop was very much closed. Try that in most western cities and they wouldn't last long.

In search of the past and to escape Basrah's consumer society, we headed to the Basrah Museum, housed in a former palace of Saddam Hussein, overlooking the waters of the Shatt al-Arab. But it hasn't been there very long and its story is a tragic one. The original museum, in an old Ottoman *shanasheel* house in Old Basrah, was looted and closed after the 1991 Gulf War, then occupied by squatters after the 2003 invasion. Tragically, while resisting eviction in 2005, the squatters shot and killed the museum's director, and it was not until some years later that the new director successfully pushed for a new home for the museum in Saddam's palace.

The museum is reached by a long, dusty road which leads to a fortress-like guardian arch, and we arrived to see armed soldiers milling around, but there's nothing unusual about that in Iraq. One demanded our passports, no receipt offered, before waving us on, but passing under the arch we walked straight into a panicked scene of ricocheting shouts as military trucks skidded in circles of swirling dust before roaring off towards the invisible museum in the hazy distance. Eyes wide, we froze, and seconds passed before we swiftly turned, retrieved our passports from the vanishing soldier, and bolted. No questions asked. Later, a local man, now resident in Sweden, told us the museum zone is home to different militias, and that skirmishes between them are frequent. 'DON'T go there!' he insisted. How right he was. Interestingly, we crossed paths with the Swede several times in different parts of Basrah. A coincidence?

Undaunted though, the following day we launched a second assault on the museum, via an entrance where Istiklal Street ends in a rutted dusty mess. An arched entrance was indeed there, but it was overwhelmingly barricaded, blocked by massive concrete slabs and an abundance of razor-wire. As we stood there vaguely contemplating the possibilities of breaching the concrete barrier, a heavily armed soldier appeared at the gateway of a nearby villa, gun at the ready and loudly questioning our presence. Save for making an amphibian approach, there was clearly no hope. We gave up.

Sindbad Island was an easier option. And who could resist an island called Sindbad? We walked there via back-roads from the Basrah train station, following old train tracks until they vanished into the sand and rubbish, then onward through an end-of-the-world wasteland of poverty, rubble, unfinished homes, and endless sand, a world washed with shades of grey and beige until a tomato truck passed us with a blast of colour, and tramping on we came to the main road where trucks were kicking up gales of dust. Cows were calmly clustered in the midst of the traffic before we crossed a modern bridge and descended, finally, to the long narrow island in the middle of the Shatt al-Arab. Sindbad Island was not what I expected. It had once reverberated with a vibrant nightlife of dancing, drinking, gambling and entertainment. But the good times fled during the first Gulf War in 1991, little remains of the island's heady days of pleasure, and the only movement amongst the desolation is windblown rubbish, fishermen and picnickers quietly enjoying the solitude. Waterless, but awash with rubbish, the cracked remains of a large concrete fountain stand lonely among struggling weeds. An aura of time-blown sadness lingers, and only the great, empty, shell-shocked cinema stands witness to the past.

*

By day we wandered at whim, discovering a Chaldean Church, in pristine condition, well tended by a caretaker but without a congregation. It was a ghost church. An old *shanasheel* home in the Al-Ashar souq had long ago belonged to a Jewish family, back in the day, before politics and lunacy set in. Where were they all now? Gone with the winds of war, I imagine.

We met the warmest of people and witnessed astonishing sights. At the Fairuz Cake Shop the Iranian owner lavished us with a selection of creamy delicacies, literally forcing one into Peter's astonished and open mouth. On Istiklal Street an enormous bulldozer with a military escort roared up and down the road, and elsewhere a military convoy rumbled towards the Corniche, with soldiers in swivelling 'pulpits', AK47s aimed at traffic and pedestrians. 'Turrets?', I hear you say, but a pulpit is a place to be preached from, and soldiers in turrets are definitely sending out a message.

One morning we awoke fearfully to crackling, thundering sounds. A bomb? An explosion? This is Iraq, after all, but no, it was just thunder, lightning and splattering rain.

In the evenings we soothed our souls with walks along the Corniche and a short boat ride on the Shatt al-Arab's smooth waters, our faces joyful in the light of a silvery moon. We dined on street-side kebabs, delicious and tender, while the streets glowed from the red-hot coals of huge circular fire-pits where flattened fish are grilled in vertical grilling baskets.

Street-side fish barbecue

We played backgammon in cafes filled with young men passionately disputing the rules of *tawla* and dominoes, and received open-armed welcomes wherever we went. Apart from the museum.

Deciding to venture north to Al-Qurnah, where the Euphrates and Tigris gracefully join forces and become the Shatt al-Arab, we turned in circles looking for the right minibus. Eventually Peter was brutally dragged by a well-meaning man to the bus garage, culminating in a near brawl between taxi and minibus drivers, but terrified of the lunacy of yellow Dodge taxis, we jumped into a Starex minibus. I sat scrunched in a tiny space next to two enormous women in ballooning *abayas* like bulging black beanbags as the driver sped along the deserted road, past palm groves to the small town of Al-Qurnah by the confluence of the Tigris and the Euphrates, the confluence of history. A young student, Muhammad, insisted on walking us there, and after posing for photos we sat sipping tea at a small cafe overlooking the confluence. Large tourist boats sedately followed the reedy banks of the Tigris, while smaller ones zoomed madly against the current, music blaring, with young lads dancing wildly, Arabic style. Fun was in their souls.

Not far away a low-slung pontoon bridge crossed the Euphrates, and I risked arrest by taking secret photos of cars easing their way gently across the undulating bridge. It was a happy day, and very moving to stand at the meeting place of these two rivers which have played such an important role in history.

Wandering back to the bus station through small streets, we received astonished looks, passed the crumbling remains of arches and old homes, and avoided a group of armed soldiers who were invading a local park. At the bus station we were hauled into a military checkpoint where we perched on a soldier's bed as our passports were perused, and were released just as the leaden skies opened. As heavy rain thundered down we leapt onto a minibus with a silver-haired driver, who, unlike wild young *shebab*, drove cautiously on the slippery road as he pointed his bus towards Basrah. It had been a day with a bit of everything: drama, history, sunshine, rain, warm encounters.

That night there was an urgent rap on our door – it was the hotel receptionist informing Peter he must move to a single room. What?? A long discussion ensued…. a police check was imminent, unmarried couples could not share a room, Peter must move. Utterly frustrated with the absurdity of having just spent five days in the same room without question, Peter declared in **indignant** tones that I was his sister, and in any case we were leaving the following day. Mollified, they accepted that. And back to sleep we went.

*

Our final day in Basrah, and we roamed the old Al-Ashar souq discovering a treasure trove of old *shanasheel* buildings hidden behind modern hoardings, and much older buildings possibly dating back centuries. I was drawn by a grimy shop window jumbled with dust-covered items, treasures and junk, and stepped in to meet the eccentric owner. Repairing a mobile phone at his workbench he was surrounded by trinkets, sculptures, Buddha heads, a picture of Jesus, prayer beads, old cassette players, jewellery, old walking sticks, books, clocks and more. His English was good and as we talked he was delighted to show me a silver ring with a piece of engraved amber. Ancient, he said, but so small I couldn't decipher the engraving. With a head of snowy hair and a wiry white beard fanning out sideways he himself looked like an antique remnant from another era. I don't doubt that amongst the clutter there were indeed treasures, but who would be buying them? The shop's wooden door frame was warped, the glass in the door badly cracked, and everything spoke of better days, long gone. I took his photo and looking at him now, with his deeply furrowed brow, I see a far away look in his eyes, a look of sorrow, and gentle resignation. This is Iraq.

Meanwhile, plans are underway to clean up the canals and restore some of Basrah's architectural treasures, and down by the Shatt, music, joyful screams and flashes of colour from a funfair light the evening sky. I like to think hope is in the air too.

*

We had tickets for first class seats on the train to Baghdad that night, and at the station, while waiting for a playful sniffer dog to clear the long line of passengers' bags, we chatted to a bubbly young Baghdadi woman. She was an interior designer working on a project in Basrah, and proudly showed us photos of her work - conformist replicas of the latest chic but sterile fads to be seen in any glossy home decor magazine in the west. With Iraq's rich architectural and cultural history surely there is potential to at least fuse past designs with modern, creating an elegant and original nod to the past. For a brief moment I probably had a faraway look of resignation in my eyes too.

As the train pulled out of Basrah at 7.30 PM on the dot, we sat upright in our worn, red upholstered seats watching, riveted, as the dark night glowed red. The memories remain, as vivid as those flares lighting the night sky.

***

On the platform, Basrah Train Station

***

Early morning at the Malwiya Minaret

7

SAMARRA

Picked up at 8.00 AM by a smartly dressed driver in a silver VW, we drove through the streets of Baghdad below a misty sky tinged with dust and alive with the twists and turns of a zillion pigeons. An early morning chill sharpened the air, people were rugged up in coats and hoodies. Blue domes shimmered softly in the haze, a gentle breeze ruffled trees overhanging modern bus shelters in abstract designs, and palm-tree brickwork decorated government buildings. This was the chic area west of the Tigris.

We were off to Samarra to visit the ninth-century Malwiya Minaret and Great Mosque, one of Iraq's better known tourist attractions. For the first time in Iraq we had booked a car and driver as we had heard too many stories of others doing it alone in shared taxis, and being denied entrance. No point in risking our lives on a wild two hour ride for nothing. We had specifically requested a silver-haired driver, generally more cautious than younger daredevil types, but though our man was young and not silver-haired, he was calm, respected the speed limit, wore a seat-belt and said very little. He drove carefully, the road was in good condition and all was well. We actually relaxed.

Samarra, 125 kilometres north of Baghdad, became the new capital of the Abbasid empire in 836 AD and during the following decade lavish palaces and the Great Mosque of Samarra rose from the desert sands. Alas the city's moment of glory was short-lived as it flourished for less than sixty years, until Baghdad reclaimed the title of capital in 892, leaving Samarra in decline, although it remained a centre of trade.

Interestingly, because it was largely abandoned in the ninth century it was spared the endless layers of new construction overlaying the old, and to this day retains its original city plan and legacy of unique Islamic architecture, decorative mosaics and carvings. It is now considered guardian of the sole remaining physical traces of the Abbasid Caliphate when at its peak.

From the 10th century, Samarra became a centre of pilgrimage for its Shia shrines, and the Al-Aksari Mosque, built in 944 and still surviving, is one of the holiest shrines in the world for Shia Muslims. It apparently survived the onslaught of Hulagu, the grandson of Genghis Khan, when he rampaged through the city in 1278, destroying many of Samarra's lavish buildings after laying waste to Baghdad twenty years earlier. And so the centuries passed, alternating between peace and violence. In the 18th century Samarra witnessed battles between Ottomans and Persians, and in 2003 US-led forces swept through, using the Malwiya Minaret as a watchtower. The surroundings saw military clashes and operations, followed by rising tensions between Shia and the largely Sunni population, and for a period ISIS controlled large parts of the Saladin Governorate, which includes Samarra. Between 2007 and 2014 insurgents attacked the Al-Aksari Mosque, toppling the dome and minarets with a series of bomb blasts and triggering riots and reprisals across Iraq. ISIS attacked the city in 2014, causing further damage to holy sites. But the Al-Aksari Mosque, which is close to the Malwiya Minaret, has since been repaired and as we passed it with its golden dome once more glittering in the midday sun, a clutter of busses were disgorging hundreds of black clad pilgrims on their way to pay homage to the bodies of the imams within.

With its troubled past and the fragile present, Samarra remains a city of huge importance for Shia, and is still very much on high alert. Security is taken very seriously and it is not surprising that checkpoints, controlled not by the Iraqi government, but by Shia militia, line the roads into the city. At the time we visited it was impossible for foreigners to enter the city proper, and we were allowed to visit only the Malwiya Minaret and the Grand Mosque.

Two hours after leaving Baghdad we arrived at the outskirts of Samarra, and stopping at a traffic light were shocked speechless by our first vision of the famous spiral minaret. After passing through checkpoint after interminable checkpoint, there it was, across the intersection and rising from behind a wall painted in the red, white and black stripes of the Iraqi flag. We gaped. For it was vastly diminished in size, and decidedly shabby. The photos we had seen had clearly exaggerated its height and a ghastly feeling of disappointment hit both of us, along with total bewilderment. Until it dawned, slowly, that we were looking at a mini-model of the minaret. It had fooled us both and, hugely relieved, we screamed with laughter at the unintended practical joke.

The checkpoints continued, one after another, **like trials testing us before finally being deemed worthy of casting our eyes on that most magnificent of edifices.**

And oh what joy when the real vision hovered into site! Even from a distance the spiralling Malwiya Minaret is absolutely stunning. The shocking disappointment of the mini-minaret imposter only highlighted the beauty of the real thing.

Obliged to leave our passports with soldiers at the final checkpoint, we were dropped at a roundabout near the entrance to the mosque's compound, leaving our driver to nap in the shade of nearby trees.

Close up the minaret rises regally from the desert sands, its beige brickwork soft against the bluest of skies, an image of timeless majesty emphasising that we humans at its base are nothing but insignificant and passing moments in time. The compound's entrance offers information boards in English detailing the history and structure of the mosque and minaret, which would no doubt be fascinating if only it was comprehensible.

I'm still baffled by its claim that Samarra belongs to the 'era quilts (5,000-4,500 BC)'. Quilts?

We were the only visitors and in mad excitement we photographed each other jumping in sheer joy with the minaret soaring behind us, capturing the unforgettable moment in time. Then began the terrifying climb, winding slowly upwards, around and around, the ramp and steps becoming narrower the higher we went, and the views changing with each turn. It was the equivalent of being on a slow motion inverse childhood helter-skelter. It is said that Caliph Al-Mutawakkil, who had commissioned the construction of the Great Mosque and Minaret, often rode his donkey up the spiralling ramp to enjoy the view. A brave man, but I definitely felt safer with my feet and centre of gravity anchored securely to a solid surface.

On the lower levels the steps are easily wide enough for two people to pass without danger, but like a limpet I glued myself to the wall, not moving for a single soul. A metal railing is attached to the inside wall but there is nothing on the external side to stop a careless climber from plunging to the ground, far below. Gripping the handrail for dear life, I crept slowly up the spiralling well-spaced steps, vertigo lurking at the thought of relinquishing my hold until we finally reached the top via a short flight of steps through an arched tunnel, arriving at a small broken concrete platform which I resisted climbing onto for the ultimate view. But we had made it. Perching close to the unrailed edge 52 metres above ground level, we gazed out at dizzying views in every direction. For a short time we were the only people there, just us and the birds and the big blue sky. It was both exhilarating and terrifying. Looking down on the baked earth below I saw clear traces of ancient paved areas and building foundations, some marked by swirling tyre tracks in the bone dry earth. Had they been left by military vehicles doing wheelies during the war? The area had been used by US forces, so perhaps.... With other people beginning to arrive at the top it was time to leave, and cautiously descending we passed fearless Iraqi men striding up while cheerily chatting on mobile phones, and several women in flowing black *abayas*. The very idea of wearing a voluminous *abaya* on a precarious climb like that was terrifying. Ever fearful of tripping I continued to grip the railing and by the time we reached the safety of ground level my palms were rust red.

Two charming and eager to please policemen who had welcomed us to the site were still sheltering in the shade of the mosque's walls, searching online for information in English about the minaret and mosque. They proudly shared this with us before curiosity drew us away from them and off we went on a walk around the mosque's perimeter, following the walls punctuated by windows and doors, picking our way through sand, down into ditches and past piles and piles of neatly stacked old square paving tiles. Behind the mosque we found a solitary sun-bleached ram's horn in the dusty remains of excavated ruins, and through a large gateway had a framed view of the distant minaret rising heavenwards. For 400 years the mosque had been the largest in the world and could accommodate up to 80,000 worshippers until Hulagu destroyed it. As a reminder of the fickleness of glory it is now reduced to a vast empty space within its remaining walls. It must have been stunning once for it is thought the inner walls were covered with dark blue glass panels. Beyond splendid, it would have been out of this world. Past and present, rise and fall.... the name Samarra is a shortened form of the original 'Surra man ra'a', meaning 'delight for all who see it', though along the years some have changed this to 'Sa'a man ra'a', meaning 'sadness for all who see it'. In reality it was, and is, a bit of both.

Once back outside the compound we spotted several roadside stalls selling what appeared to be upside-down ice-cream cones in different sizes. Eager for a sweet treat we headed over….. to discover that the cones were in fact golden mini-replicas of the minaret. Clearly the heat and excitement had made us delirious, but given that these were the first souvenir stalls we'd seen in Iraq we could be forgiven.

We left at midday, driving back to Baghdad on an appallingly bad road in clouds of billowing dust. Road works were in full swing and the resulting track was a jarring, rutted, sandy mess. Total anarchy reigned as drivers veered on to the wrong (but sealed) side of the road, driving suicidally into near head-on collisions before veering back across to the rutted side when oncoming trucks and cars bore down upon us. It was absolutely insane. Despite doing his best to preserve his pristine car, our calm and careful driver resorted to taking risks and finally lost his cool when a cheeky minivan driver tried to push in front of us at a dangerous road crossing. Aggressive and insulting words were exchanged, our driver refused to give way, and for a moment we feared it might come to blows. It didn't, but tempers were definitely frayed and hackles rising. I'm sure at that point our driver regretted taking us to Samarra. We continued along a heavily fortified stretch of road, and as we juddered, slithered and jolted, I tried to snap illegal photos of the many mini-forts as we passed. Unsuccessfully. Closer to Baghdad the road reverted to a smoother surface and we followed a long blast-proof concrete wall for kilometres. I suspected it was concealing some kind of military installation and didn't dare raise my camera.

Three hours later, tired, battered and hungry we rolled into Baghdad's suburbs and traffic jams, hugely relieved to be back in civilisation. Suddenly Baghdad's roads and traffic seemed quite sane.

***

Mini-replica Malwiya Minaret, at the crossroads

Top: Front of the Ctesiphon Arch
Bottom: Close up of the arch

8

CTESIPHON

Another ancient destination was calling. Ctesiphon, a name with a magical ring to it.

I had never before heard of it, and I had to see it.

For over eight hundred years Ctesiphon was the royal capital of the Parthian and Sassanian empires and by the late sixth century was considered the largest city in the world. It was said to have rivalled Constantinople.

Ctesiphon was founded in the late 120s BC on the site of a military camp on the eastern bank of the Tigris, 35 kilometres southeast of Baghdad, and became the winter capital of the Parthian Empire around 58 BC. The Parthians, a major power in ancient Persia, ruled from 247 BC to 224 AD. Their empire expanded south from Persia's north-east to Mesopotamia, and at its height stretched from the headwaters of the Euphrates in central-eastern Turkey, through present day Afghanistan to Pakistan. But as the centuries passed, internal conflict and wars with Rome weakened the

Parthian Empire which gave way to the Sassanians, the final and longest lived of the Persian dynasties, which ruled for more than four centuries, from 224 AD until the Muslim conquest of Persia in 651 AD.

Well placed on the Silk Road between the Mediterranean and China, Ctesiphon flourished under the Sassanians, becoming a wealthy commercial centre. Merging with cities on both sides of the Tigris it was also known as The Cities, or al-Mada'in in Arabic. To put its size into perspective, it covered 30 square kilometres, twice the surface area of fourth-century Rome.

*

Down in the hotel's basement breakfast room Radi was suffering from a serious hangover after a drinking spree on Baghdad's night-time streets, but was nonetheless smiling and looking very snappy in his new waiter's tunic. After the usual breakfast of lentil soup, salad, and *tahina*[25] with a swirl of date syrup mopped up with fluffy flatbread, we were out of the hotel by nine o'clock. In search of a minibus to Jisr Dyala (Dyala Bridge) we set off walking to nearby Bab al Sharji, where we'd been told we could find one going south. Eventually we came across an erratic and constantly moving gathering of minibuses at the far end of Tahrir Square. The customary mayhem prevailed but after several false starts we were pushed and dragged aboard a moving, crowded minibus by helpful locals, and miraculously heading in the right direction. Through Baghdad's traffic

[25] A Middle Eastern dip made from ground, toasted sesame seeds, also used in hummus and other dishes

jams, past a mix of blackened shabby structures, and inhabited end-of-the world buildings side by side with fine new architecture, we drove through hazy smog, out of Baghdad and into the remnants of countryside, past groves of date palms and greenery which shone through the smog like surviving 'glimpses of past glory' as Peter put it. Thrown off the minibus at Jisr Dyala, we scrambled on to another one going to Salman Pak. It was all a mystery to me, but everyone aboard the buses knew where we wanted to go and pushing and shoving aside, took great care of us.

Ancient Ctesiphon, now known as Taq Kasra, is next to the town of Salman Pak, meaning Salman the Pure, and named after Salman the Persian who was a companion of the Prophet Muhammad. The town is perhaps better known for its nearby military facility, which, in the lead-up to the 2003 invasion, was falsely labelled by the US as an important centre of Iraq's biological and chemical weapon programs, as well as a terrorist training camp. No evidence has ever been produced to support these claims. To the contrary it is now believed that it was a counter terrorism training camp for army commandos.

Arriving in Salman Pak we were dropped on the main road which led to a mosque hovering at the far end. The final stretch of the road was barricaded, accessible only to pedestrians and guarded by soldiers who, when asked for directions to Taq Kasra, waved their hands towards the mosque. Seeing no sign of a soaring old arch, the only surviving remnant of the old city, we hesitated, when out of the blue a young local woman approached us, asking in perfect English if we needed help. She was *hijabed*, well dressed, heavily made up, confident, smiling and charming. And told us that Taq Kasra was in fact behind the mosque. Given that she was alone, she was astonishingly friendly and not at all shy about speaking to two foreigners, and in true Iraqi style invited us for lunch with her family. She was very insistent, and having exchanged phone numbers, called me later to reissue her invitation, but we politely refused as time was short, and on we marched, round behind the mosque, passing a strip of abandoned shops, their dark interiors littered with rubbish and rubble. Past a school with a jumble of bicycles parked in front, we continued along a dusty road until ahead of us rose what could only be the famous arch of Ctesiphon. The largest surviving free-standing, unreinforced brick arch in the world.

It was huge and magnificent, even in ruin.

Excitement was growing, but as we came closer we found the gates closed and locked, and entrance impossible. We were so tantalisingly close, but peering through the gates had only a side view of the old palace walls which are beyond thick. We could see that the arch was filled with a latticework of scaffolding, restoration work was underway and a resident guard told us the site was dangerous. Which it probably was. Nonetheless, we tried to charm our way in, but failed, though the guard suggested we ask for permission at the nearby archaeological museum. Forlornly we toddled off to the small building where we met a gaggle of men who, after furtive discussion, offered to take us in for US $25 each. A request for baksheesh, which we found a bit pricey and so refused. Nothing to do but to walk around the perimeter of the walled-off site. As we left the museum a young fresh-faced *shebab* made a sudden appearance, sporting a brown and gold Louis Vuitton waistcoat and one of those infamous electric-shock Baghdadi hairdos. Peter likened his 'coiffe' to a Great Crested Grebe and was thrilled when he was kindly allowed to touch the gelled creation. As I dragged Peter away from his Great Crested Grebe the museum men called out, warning us to keep to the road. 'There are still landmines', they said. We weren't sure if things were looking up, or not.

Peter with the Great Crested Grebe

Sticking obediently to a small sealed road which looped around behind the arch, I was vaguely contemplating crossing the scrubby, rubbish-strewn land between road and ruin when a lone, rusting sign in red Arabic appeared by the side of the road. Fortunately Peter could read it – for it warned of landmines on the south side. We had no idea where the south side was and there was no barbed wire to deter entry. Just this one solitary battered sign.

Rusting land mine warning

So with chins up we walked on, pausing from time to time to admire the massive barrel shape of the ruined palace. Birds chirped, stray dogs foraged in the scrubby vegetation and a stillness pervaded, when, like something from a hippy movie, a cheery yellow microbus jolted past us, its driver calling out 'Welcome to Iraq, welcome', before slamming on the brakes and reversing in a flurry to excitedly invite us for lunch, a chicken lunch. With great difficulty we declined. Moments later a man on a bicycle also enthusiastically invited us for lunch. This time for fish. That was the third offer of lunch within less than an hour. This is Iraq.

Still following the road we circled the palace hall, admiring it from all angles. The walls were astonishingly solid, seven metres thick at the base, and one metre thick at the top of the arch, but great jagged cracks had appeared at one side of the structure and the front wall was beginning to separate from the rest. Leaning at an alarming angle away from the main structure it had been bolstered at some stage by a great flying buttress.

The arch soars to a height of 37 metres and is winged by decorative facades at the front. Of these only the arch and the left facade are parts of the original palace complex. The other side was partially restored under Saddam Hussein in the 1980s. The open arch marks the entrance to what may have been the throne room, a barrel vaulted hall 48 metres long. It is an extraordinary structure. Seen from behind, its enclosed barrel form is absolutely massive, but in front, though equally big, it is open to the elements and more delicate, more fragile. Nobody knows the exact date of construction, but somewhere between the third and sixth centuries this marvel of engineering took shape, and incredibly it is still standing. To put the enormity of it into perspective we posed for photos with the arch rising behind us. We appear as lonely dots, backed by the soaring arch and surrounded by a wasteland of shrubby terrain, littered with dust and rubble, and a haunting feeling of desolation. It was a moving experience, knowing that over fifteen centuries this extraordinary wonder has stood watch over armies, wars, invasions and occupations. It has been used as a palace, as a mosque, had tourists crawling over the fragile arch for photos, and now stands empty, crumbling, awaiting care and restoration. I just hope it isn't too late.

In front of the arch a long straight road led to a distant building, large and forbidding - the Panorama Performing Arts Centre which stands like a multi-vaulted mausoleum, its tall windowless brick facade sweeping sheer from top to bottom like a modern version of an ancient citadel, cold and unwelcoming. Was it built by Saddam? Very little information is to be found online, other than reviews on Google Maps - reviews which bemoan the neglect and decay of the once beautiful building which embodied the battles between Iraq and Iran in a series of paintings. Abandoned after the fall of the regime and damaged by the American occupation, the paintings were burned, and the building looted and ransacked until nothing remained but the empty windowless shell. Others commented on the total darkness inside. Some reviews said it's not suitable for tourists as it contains military waste, and one bizarre comment said 'The chicks were still vomiting.' A coded message referring to the storage of military waste? After all, Salman Pak is home to that military facility which the US would have had the world believe was evil.

Had we looked in advance at an aerial view of Ctesiphon on Google Maps, we would have seen a huge number of lines in the earth tracing the foundations of significant ancient structures surrounding the arch. A little further away, behind the museum lies a maze of foundations of small rooms, and the remains of a church, the Church of Kokheh, previously a temple of the Parthian gods. Dates vary, but some sources suggest that the Church of the East[26] began here back in the late first century when Kokheh replaced the ancient city of Seleucia. However, excavations have only revealed remains from the Sassanian period, dating from the third to the end of the sixth century. No matter how old the ruins are, we had missed the opportunity to investigate further. If only we had done our homework in advance.

We didn't visit the Panorama either, but moved on back towards Salman Pak, keeping to a worn track used by school kids on bicycles as we meandered through the rubble, hoping it was free of mines. Back in the town, we stopped at a smart new juice cafe, and as we sat on the pleasant terrace enjoying a refreshing juice a man pushing his daughter in a wheelchair approached us. The teenage girl was severely crippled, both physically and mentally, he was emaciated, and my heart stopped with the horror of what his life must be like. This was not a beggar patrolling a tourist strip. There were no tourists. This was a man whose only way of survival was to ask locals for help. We gave him some dinar, though it's never enough, and walked on, sobered by the encounter.

As we came to the security checkpoint at the end of the pedestrianised street we were stopped by a burly

[26] Also known as the East Syriac Church, Persian Church, Assyrian Church, Babylon Church and Nestorian Church

soldier. In a refreshing twist it was not to see our passports, but to insist we join him for lunch. The fourth lunch invitation that day. We declined. He insisted, his insistence becoming louder, more aggressive until he literally dragged Peter into a little shed where he was offered the soldier's own hot lunch. Once more Peter politely refused, and finally, as a concession, the soldier thrust two bottles of water into Peter's hands instead, and amongst guffaws of laughter and excitement insisted on us posing for pictures with him and his fellow soldiers. One or two snaps were taken before he dashed urgently back into the shed, emerging minutes later clad in full battle kit, bulletproof vest and ammunition magazine wrapped around his broad belly, AK47 in hand. He then assumed a seriously macho stance and suitably terrifying expression for the photos. He was a delight.

Less fun was the usual rigmarole of getting a minibus back to Baghdad. Once again changing at Jisr Dyala we found ourselves squeezed into the back seats next to two men on their way to Baghdad for medical treatment. One for an eye operation. His eye was terrifyingly bloodshot and weeping, but he was chirpy and uncomplaining. A thin young Syrian woman slithered through the tightly packed seats and squeezed into the space next to me. She was severe in black, but with a smile which lit her face as she showed me photos of her young daughter, all smiles and giggles in sparkling colourful dresses. The woman was married to an Iraqi, and we can only wonder at what twists and turns of fate had brought her to Salman Pak in Iraq. And so two and a half hours passed, much of it in crawling traffic jams, seriously testing our patience. But this is Iraq and what can you do? We were dropped off not far from Tahrir Square, emerging from the bus like creaking old crones with arthritic joints before the driver did a swift u-turn and started collecting passengers for the return trip to Jisr Dyala, back through more traffic jams. We had paid peanuts for the fare, and the mind boggles at how many trips a day the driver would have to make in order to earn a liveable profit. We in the west have absolutely nothing to complain about.

***

Dwarfed by the Ctesiphon Arch

Top: Side view of leaning front wall
Below: Walls beyond thick

At the Salman Pak checkpoint

Choli Minaret, Erbil

9

ERBIL

The road from Baghdad to Erbil, capital of the autonomous region of Kurdistan, is 360 kilometres long, straight and mostly flat. Google Maps gives the travel time of four hours fifty-two minutes, presumably at the legal speed and without stopping for lunch or at the interminable checkpoints and border post. We did it in a suicidal five hours, including all stops. Unusually, there are white lines marking the lanes which should add a certain safety, but as drivers speed, weaving in and out between other cars, fearlessly taking terrifying risks the lines don't really serve for much, other than to mark the centre as the perfect place for vendors to set up stalls.

*

Never ones to miss breakfast, we downed the usual fare and farewelled Radi with smiles, handshakes, and a definite sadness before grabbing a taxi to the Nahda Bus and Taxi Terminal less than three kilometres north-east of the hotel. The terminal is a large modern complex heaving with the raucous shouts of men with foghorn voices touting different destinations, revving of engines and the constant ebb and flow of yellow taxis swarming like bees, and sleekly brutish GMCs lording it tank-like over the smaller cars.

Nahda means 'the Awakening' in Arabic, and was used to refer to a cultural movement that flourished in Arab areas dominated by the Ottoman Empire during the late 19th and early 20th centuries. Clearly a special time in the history of Arab resistance to colonisers, but why the bus and taxi terminal should be called the Awakening is a mystery to me. An awakening, or revival of freedom to travel, perhaps.

On arrival and not yet out of our taxi, we were pounced upon by young touts scouting for business for the wildly-chauffeured yellow Dodge taxis. Or more precisely, Dodge Chargers. Not only did they dodge oncoming traffic with suicidal daring, they also charged like wild stallions racing along the length and breadth of Iraq's highways. Not for us, we shook them off and marched purposefully off to the line reserved for GMCs, where we were ushered straight into one bound for Erbil. No time to pause for thought or to seek out another one with a silver-haired driver. Peter remembers the driver as being relatively youngish, with a military style haircut and a nightclub bouncer air to him. In we went, squashed into the last available, and the most uncomfortable, seats at the back, three of us sharing seats meant for two, with luggage pressing against our heads from behind and where even my short little legs felt cramped. Straddling two seats with a gap between them, and with his long legs folded up so that his knees pointed skywards, Peter suffered horribly. And instantly regretted stepping into this taxi as soon as he saw the driver's face in the rear view mirror.

We pulled out of Nahda Garage at 9.45 AM, bracing ourselves for the five and a half hour trip north. The driver started out well enough but that suicidal Iraqi madness soon kicked in when he decided to make a video call to a friend, and the terror began. Screaming down the road at 150 kilometres an hour, he chatted and laughed, alternating between gazing at the screen of his phone which lay beside him and casting the briefest of glances at the road ahead. This went on for a good hour. It was hell. And absolutely terrifying, though I was grateful to be at the back and unable to see the reality of what lay ahead on the road. Not far north of Baghdad the road passed by Baqubah, capital of Diyala Governorate which still has issues with insurgents. We had read about a recent attack on a nearby village and so hunkered down, dragging scarves over our heads in an absurd attempt to make ourselves inconspicuous. If anything we were probably drawing attention to our foreignness…. after all, this had never worked at a checkpoint.

We flew along the long flat desert road, surviving total anarchy with cars blithely driving on the wrong side as lunatics challenged oncoming traffic to a game of chicken. This is Iraq.

Racing steadily north under dusty, cloudy skies, after a

few hours we mercifully stopped for lunch at a large restaurant complex where a large military convoy was parked, and our driver and fellow passengers dined on hearty kebabs and rice. We perched on benches outside, munching on sandwiches stuffed with boiled eggs and watching a team of young men hosing and cleaning the desert dust from our GMC. With everyone refreshed and with frozen joints loosened we piled back into our rabbit hutch seats and continued along the highway, only slowing down at small insignificant settlements where men and women had planted small stalls slap bang in the middle of the road, selling bananas, coffee, or bottles of water. I can't imagine who in their right minds would pause there, let alone stop. There were, of course, the usual security checkpoints too. An endless nuisance.

Arriving at the border between Federal Iraq and the autonomous region of Kurdistan, I expected to find just another checkpoint, so was taken aback to find an unexpectedly serious border scenario, with special lanes for customs to check luggage and a building with a multitude of immigration windows, as though we were entering a totally new country. Which of course we were, as it turned out. Our passports had to be checked but finding the correct counter for foreigners, if there was one, was not easy. Counters were numbered but nothing was written in English and communication was a problem. Not even the scrum of Iraqis seemed to know what was happening, and we floundered, until two of our fellow passengers, Eyad, from Mosul and another man from Basrah took pity on us, kindly helping direct us from one window to another. Time after time we were redirected by unfriendly, unsmiling and unhelpful Kurdish officials. The clock was ticking. While Peter and I were desperately trying to negotiate the immigration counters, back at the GMC the customs officials were ransacking our luggage, showing special interest, as I would later discover, in the small bag where I kept my knickers, and leaving neatly packed clothes in total disorder. I was not impressed. Eventually, after pushing my way to the head of a queue at an open window, I handed over our passports which were duly photographed, handed back and with a nod we were off. Looking back, we recall that nothing was stamped in our passports, no paper was given. Could we have got away without bothering with it all?

On we went into darkening clouds, drizzling rain and heavy showers as the road climbed slightly through a line of hills topped with familiar mini-forts. It was a relief to see that our driver had abandoned video calls and was now paying attention to the road which was decidedly wet and slippery. Flares from distant oil fields flickered through the mist and it seemed that every fuel station we passed, and there were many, had a different name. In Kurdish. We were in serious oil country.

We knew we were close to the end when, at a discreet sign from the driver we all passed our 30,000 dinar fares forward through hands reaching out as in a relay handover, and as we drove into the outer suburbs of Erbil I began to experience the first symptoms of culture shock. Road signs became more frequent and modern buildings screaming of wealth lined the wide, multi-lane roads. I felt like we'd arrived in an alien land.

At 3.15 PM, five and a half hours and twelve checkpoints after leaving Baghdad, we were dropped by the roadside in a bland, sterile outer suburb, our bags were thrown unceremoniously to the ground from the GMC and the driver roared off without a word of farewell, nor time for a thank you from us. The other passengers had vanished like *djinns* into thin air and we were left standing, stunned and puzzled, along with Eyad our friend from Mosul. We had grabbed our bags, ready to go in search of a taxi when Eyad pointed to a solitary remaining bag sitting on the roadside. 'Is this yours?' he asked. It wasn't. Whoever it belonged to was yet another Iraqi mystery, and so we too left, leaving the lonesome bag abandoned in the gutter. I still wonder if anyone eventually retrieved it. Eyad, a student, was an angel. He flagged down a taxi, negotiated a decent fare for us, and insisted on accompanying us to our hotel before continuing on to his home in Erbil. His refusal to accept our money for the fare resulted in a battle which we won as Peter finally thrust a handful of cash into his top pocket. He was adorable, gentle, helpful and hospitable. As we sped along the pristinely clean roads of modern Erbil, passing manicured parks and stopping at red traffic lights, I gazed around at the unfamiliar surroundings of this wealthy new city. I was already missing Iraq.

We checked into the Soul Mate Hotel, a tall, narrow and recently opened place managed by Syrians who were eager to please, charming and polite. Our room was rather chic by our usual standards, and overlooking the road it treated us to night time extravaganzas of colourful lighting playing endlessly across facades of nearby high-rise buildings, and during the early morning witching hours was punctuated by prolonged outbursts of howling dogs.

We were midway between the outer ring road and the ancient Citadel which marks the city centre, just over three kilometres and a 40-minute walk from the hotel. So before darkness fell we set off at a brisk trot towards the old Citadel and all was well until we came to a busy road with six lanes of fast flowing traffic and no sign of a pedestrian overpass or traffic lights. So we did the normal thing and stepped out to cross it. Alas, unlike Baghdad where that's the norm and cars will slow down for you, this was verging on suicidal. Not only does traffic move faster in Erbil, the cars do not slow down for you. It's a miracle that we made it across safely, and absurdly, just a few hundred metres further on was a set of traffic lights complete with pedestrian lights too. You live and you learn, or you die doing so. In the evenings a uniformed traffic policeman lurked by the intersection roadside, waving a large red wand which drivers respected. He also reprimanded us for crossing against the red light. How different to Iraq where the police stopped the traffic for us.

By the time we arrived at the base of the Citadel the evening air was perfumed with smoke from barbecuing meat, and we stopped for a kebab and salad at one of a string of street-side food stalls. Families promenaded past, enjoying the evening, the food and music. It was very much a party atmosphere, and with so many women out and about wearing colourful clothes and with their long, dark hair freely flowing, Erbil's evening streets contrasted starkly with our experience in Baghdad.

The Citadel, overshadowing Erbil's old town

Perched atop an ovoid shaped tell, the Citadel rose above us. Reaching 32 metres above street level, it covers 102,000 square metres and has been occupied for around 6,000 years, perhaps longer. Its original fortifications had given way to a wall of 19th-century façades which still give the impression of a fortress, though I was disappointed at the outward looking windows which no self-respecting fortress should have.

Circling the Citadel's base until the road quietened, we entered its dark side, with no street food, no tourists, closed shops and very little street lighting. But we found a steep ramp leading upwards to the Citadel's plateau, and through a gateway entrance we followed a straight street lined with 19th-century buildings. All closed and slightly ghostly. In a small amphitheatre behind the wall overlooking the party street below, we stumbled across several Russian actors practising for an avant garde performance for a cultural event. They were not happy to be interrupted by a man with a booming voice trying to make conversation with us.

Inside, most of the buildings and urban plan date back to the 19th-century Ottoman period, but since then many buildings have been destroyed, others suffered from neglect and were considered dangerous, and in 2007 a restoration project was announced and all the inhabitants, save one family, were evicted. Unsurprisingly, that solitary family too has moved on. Without shops or everyday facilities life must have become too difficult, or perhaps living amongst the ghostly memories was too much. There are now plans for fifty families to live in the Citadel once it is renovated, but will that be for the original inhabitants, or for specially selected members of the upper levels of Kurdish society? I wonder.

There are some fine old homes and beautiful architecture which have been preserved, though they were closed to the public when we returned during the daytime. We did, however, spend an interesting time visiting the small Turkmen museum in an old courtyard house where photos, fabrics and everyday utensils from previous eras recreated a vanished lifestyle. It was charming and the quietly spoken guardian was clearly proud of his history. Despite this I had mixed feelings about the Citadel, fearing that in contrast to the old souq which has combined old and new, locals and tourists, and is still very much a part of everyday life, it risked becoming a museum for tourists, and without the usual clutter and energy of everyday life, a manicured ghost town.

Meanwhile the Citadel continues to dominate the city and from there all roads fan outwards, intersected by ever widening concentric roads. Erbil, or Hawler (pronounced Howler) in Kurdish, has long been a circular city and from the air it's quite a vision. At ground level, it can be confusing - if you get it wrong you can unwittingly turn in circles.

We spent several days exploring Erbil and at first I was not seduced by its clean streets and modern facade. Though the Kurds are friendly and welcoming, they are less exuberant and more reserved than the Iraqi Arabs. But slowly it began to grow on me. We sat for an entire Friday afternoon on a bench in the central square below the Citadel, watching masses of people promenading, enjoying the sunshine, drinking coffee and tea and shopping for clothes and shoes at a second-hand market. Out of the blue an astonishing image of Spiderman emerged. Wrapped from head to toe in a red and blue glove-like costume, he was selling giant pink fairy floss, or candy floss in the UK, and all kinds of toys and trinkets to attract children. He also had competition from a Panda Man and Mickey Mouse in black and white costumes, and we were entertained by all three of them for quite some time. At one point Spiderman removed his mask for some fresh air and we discovered they were Bangladeshis, trying to make a living in Kurdistan, and proof that the ancient web of trade and movement across the continent is alive and well.

I bought coffee poured from a traditional Arabic coffee pot, only to find it was Nescafe, so to find the real thing we dropped into the Machko Chai Khana, a tea house clinging to the base of the Citadel's walls, which for seventy-five years has served as a meeting place for intellectuals and activists. Its interior walls are covered with photos of local and foreign politicians, the traditional décor is colourful, cosy, charming and welcoming, and its customers include both men and women along with tourists. But it was not cheap, as we found out when we were charged an exorbitant price for an unasked-for bowl of nuts casually placed on the table.

We moved on and later, by chance, came across another more down-to-earth cafe in the bowels of the old souq. The walls and vaulted ceiling of the Maman Tea House were plastered with photos of Kurdistan's traditional life, local and historical figures. Kurdish men with great bristling moustaches and heads topped with black and white scarves wound into turbans, sat on the carpeted benches and leaned against the walls. Proud, macho, serious and fierce they were all wearing waistcoats over long-sleeved shirts, the traditional baggy, black trousers, and wide floral sashes wrapped around broad waistlines. One old man sat with his shepherd's crook between his knees. Crowded and buzzing with noise, the ambience was wonderful. We found ourselves sitting next to an Iraqi businessman and his young son from Al Diwanyeh, a town halfway between Baghdad and Nasiriyah. He insisted on offering us tea and his direct and open friendliness was refreshing.

From the main street the souq appears to have been recently built, its new cream brickwork mimicking an older design. But the further we delved into its jumbled, sparkling, messy depths, the more I felt its ancient past. Seduced by a soap seller's mellifluous voice I bought beautiful olive oil soap made in Aleppo in Syria, and was thrilled to know that trade between the two countries is still alive. Narrow, poorly lit alleyways were home to specific trades, as they have always been in this part of the world. In the afternoon tailors snoozed on piles of fabrics in their small, cluttered, vaulted shops, and looking up I saw the old dark stained brickwork of walls and overhead domes which spoke of centuries past. It was a place to lose yourself in. It was wonderful.

Leaving the souq we met Muhammad, a young student who invited us to tea in his family home opposite the famous 12th-century Choli Minaret, also known as the Broken Minaret as at some point over the centuries it had lost its top. Muhammad was delighted to practise

English, and as we sat on a swing seat draped with drying underwear in the courtyard, his mother and sisters one by one emerged from their traditional home, bursting with smiles and curiosity as we sipped the offered tea. It was a beautiful moment and a brief insight into family life in Kurdistan. Interestingly, Muhammad identified as a Turkmen, the third largest ethnic group in Iraq. Though his mother was Kurdish, his father was of Turkmen origin, a descendant of Turkic migration passing through on the way to Mesopotamia between the seventh and early twentieth centuries. When his father returned, clearly taken aback to see us in his home, he offered the briefest of greetings before disappearing. He wasn't happy to see us, and unwilling to upset things, we didn't linger long.

Behind the souq lies a small area of ancient buildings and winding streets which we wandered into by chance. Most of the buildings are abandoned, many are lined with great jagged fissures, or blackened by fire. But peering through open windows I caught glimpses of a better past in the tangle of overgrown courtyards. Nobody could tell us what had happened here, but I like to think that the government will find a way to preserve what must be a significant part of Erbil's history.

Erbil has some large parks which are airy, green oases, perfect for escaping the cars and noise. The Sami Abdul Rahman Park is the largest, covering two square kilometres of greenery, including lakes, a rose garden and even a plantation of eucalyptus trees. It was created on the site of a former Saddam era military base, and in memory of those who fought for Kurdish freedom from Iraqi rule there is a monument with the inscription, 'Freedom is not free', for the Kurds suffered terribly from Saddam's reprisals after collaborating against him during the 1980 to 1988 Iran-Iraq war. Casualties from the resulting Kurdish genocide number somewhere between 50,000 and 200,000. The park was pleasant and calm in the late afternoon chill, very few people were there though a group of rowdy tourists in an electric buggy came dangerously close as they swept past us. Like old ladies we sat on a bench overlooking a lake, watching the autumnal light on the water until dusk, before scuttling back to the hotel.

For something with a historical twist the Minarah Park offers a long avenue lined with the busts of numerous Kurdish leaders and important citizens, including a giant statue of Ibn al-Mustawfi, a 12th/13th-century historian born in Erbil's Citadel. A woman had somehow climbed up and onto the statue and sat cross-legged, looking every bit a Lilliputian as she pretended to read the huge book in Mustawfi's lap while her husband photographed her. I considered clambering up for a photograph too, but the climb was deceptively daunting. In the same park we posed next to mini-replicas of Erbil's monuments - I have a photo of Peter towering over the Citadel, while I dwarfed the Broken Minaret.

With Peter determined to send postcards from Kurdistan we made two abortive trips to the Post Office to buy stamps. The first time it was closed when we arrived, and the second time, after smiles and welcomes from workers who seemed to have nothing better to do, we were told that yes, they could sell him stamps, very beautiful stamps, but he would have to send the postcards by DHL at additional cost. We learned, in fact, that the Iraqi government had basically stopped the regular mail service in Kurdistan. Posting those cards turned into quite an ordeal for Peter who lovingly carried them with him to Luxor in Egypt where the post office happily sold him a collection of stamps. Alas they were so big, and numerous, that they would have covered both sides of the cards including addresses and message. So he bought an envelope at a shop across the road, but even that was barely big enough for all the stamps. And in the end nobody ever received the cards.

On our last day in Erbil, on a whim we walked to the city's outer limits, through kilometres of high-rise buildings under construction, just to sip juice in the eccentric Furry Cat Cafe where cats of all shapes and sizes, rescued and donated, lived together in the marble-floored space of a converted shop run by a Syrian family. One of the cats took a violent dislike to my earrings, lashing out at lightning speed. I was not impressed and in turn took an instant dislike to the not so furry feline. Peter however had a lovely time cuddling friendlier cats until we were asked to leave when our allotted hour was up. I'm not sure if cat cafes are a new trend in the world, but it was the last thing I expected to see in Iraq. Or rather, in Erbil.

Preparing for his departure to Egypt Peter decided to

spruce up before leaving the country, and drawn to a salon staffed by young Syrian men he had his hair cut and ears cleaned as he reclined in the barber's chair, a cotton bud embedded in each ear and held in place by a terrifying spring contraption. I thought about asking them to cut my hair too, but decided it was safer to sit and sip the juice which the lads had kindly offered me.

Erbil had offered a rest from the mayhem of federal Iraq, a place to recuperate and digest the whirlwind days of the past three weeks. But I wanted one last burst of Iraqi energy, and Mosul was calling.

***

Back street in old Erbil

Spiderman and fairy floss, in the square below the Citadel

The ruins of Mosul's once-beautiful old city

10

MOSUL

Mosul, on the banks of the Tigris around 400 kilometres north of Baghdad, grew out of the ruins of the ancient city of Nineveh, capital of the Assyrians. Settled as far back as 6,000 BC, Nineveh was one of the most significant cities in antiquity, and such is the power of its memory that its name is still used today for the part of Mosul on the eastern banks of the river. With a population of close to 4 million, it is the second largest city in Iraq.

The name Mosul, or Mawsil, means 'linking point' in Arabic and, due to its strategic location at a junction of trade routes, it has long been a centre of international commerce. Its diverse population includes Arabs, Assyrians, Turkmens, Kurds, and other ethnic minorities. It has also been affectionately called *al-Faih*, Paradise, and The Pearl of the North, names which hint at its ancient beauty. One of the more historically and culturally significant cities of the Arab world, Mosul was famed in the 13th century for luxury brass items inlaid with silver, and is also known for its local alabaster, known as 'Mosul marble'. Sunni Islam is the predominant religion, and until 2003 Mosul was home to a significant Christian community, but by the time ISIS arrived 50,000 Christians had fled and since then few have returned.

From the Assyrians in the 25th century BC to modern day ISIS, the city has been ruled by an endless stream of empires and invaders. It has been destroyed, rebuilt, and witnessed untold battles, most recently the destruction by ISIS and carpet bombing of the old city by US-led coalition forces.

*

Straddling the Tigris, Mosul is only 84 kilometres north-west of Erbil, but reluctant to participate in what might be seen as ogling at misfortune we had hesitated to go there. Disaster tourism is not my usual thing. But the longer we stayed in the wealthy sterility of Erbil, the more I yearned to return to Iraq, and Mosul was just a little over an hour's drive away. We really shouldn't miss it, and I nagged at Peter until he agreed.

So with an early start from the bus station in Erbil, we climbed into a minibus for a wild ride to the city which had suffered years of violence following the 2003 invasion, including numerous suicide bombings, occupation by ISIS and eventual liberation in 2017 at an enormous human cost when the old city, home to a million people, was heavily bombed, with further damage resulting from improvised explosives left behind by a fleeing ISIS. During the nine-month battle to liberate Mosul from ISIS, US-led coalition and Iraqi forces battered the old city, in the process razing it and killing up to 11,000 civilians, many of them crushed by the buildings they were sheltering in. Buildings they were *told* to shelter in when the Iraqi government dropped and distributed leaflets advising people to stay put. On top of that thousands were killed by ISIS, and are buried in mass graves. I had seen photos of the damage, I had heard the stories, and I asked myself why would I want to witness the remnants of such horror. Curiosity, yes. But more than that it was a need to know, to understand something so far from my experience of life that it seemed immoral to bury my head in the sand.

Even before entering Mosul proper we passed buildings which were still reeling from bombs dropped years before. Crumpled, shattered, uninhabitable homes and shops dotted the road until we entered the city through a gap in the 3,000 year-old crenellated and partially restored walls of Nineveh. Though ISIS had destroyed much of the ancient ruins, behind these walls there are still archaeological remains and ironically, new discoveries have recently been revealed because of the destruction. In 2022, while restoring the ISIS damaged Mashki Gate of Nineveh, archaeologists unearthed marble slabs covered with Assyrian carvings and cuneiform writing. Buried and unnoticed for centuries they had survived ISIS's bulldozers. A small miracle.

But we were there to visit the parts of the city where most of the destruction had taken place in 2017, so dropped just inside the old walls, we took a taxi to the old city. And I was totally unprepared for that first vision of the ruins. We were crossing a bridge from the east to the west side of the Tigris, and there, across the river and to the right, was a sight which will be forever imprinted on my memory. Spotlit in the sunshine the jagged crumbled ruins of old Mosul sloping down to the river were like something from an earthquake scene. It took me a moment to comprehend what I was looking at.

Our taxi driver left us at the entrance to a fish market just after the Old Bridge, and walking through the newly covered market, past stands of fresh fish, we came to the end, where the shattered remains of destruction loomed large. A wasteland confronted us with the surreal sight of a few remaining buildings dotting the rubble, standing stoically as they had done for centuries. We stopped, and a man in his late 60s, tall, with a white skull cap on his head, and a beige military-style waistcoat over a black *dishdash*[27] approached us. 'You can't enter', he said, 'the bulldozers are in there. You'll have to come back later.' What were they clearing? Rubble, and looking for unexploded bombs.

As we talked to Hussein, he led us away down alternative back streets and we spent the next few hours with him, walking past extraordinary scenes of piles of rubble interspersed with visions of beautiful interior

[27] Long robe with long sleeves, worn in Arab countries

decoration in surviving but inaccessible rooms. A two-storey building, painted pink and inexplicably unscathed, rose to our right. People were still living there, surrounded by mounds of rubble. Many of the buildings had 'safe' written in both Arabic and English painted on the walls, indicating that these buildings and ruins had been checked and declared safe from hidden explosives. The occasional scrap of colourful fabric lay half buried in the rubble, a battered couch perched at an angle on broken concrete. We walked on as Hussein spoke about what had happened here. 'People were told to stay at home,' he said. And so of course they were crushed as their homes collapsed around them when the B52s dropped their bombs. Tons of bombs. Hussein was angry, had been warned by authorities not to talk about these things, but what did he have to lose. He'd already lost his home. And if he didn't speak the truth, then who would. On we walked as he pointed out remains of homes, naming the families who had lived there. Past a convent, beyond repair but with a garden where a neighbouring woman in a still intact house often went. Bursting with positive energy despite living in a disaster zone, she invited us for tea which we refused for Hussein was keen to move on. I peered through a hole in the corrugated iron fence and saw tall grass and weeds sprouting amongst the shattered concrete and stones. Would we like to go in? asked the woman. She had the key. We declined and looking back I'm glad we did, for how could we be sure it had been properly cleaned of insidiously hidden explosives? Mosul is not a place to step lightly off the main track.

We meandered on the heels of Hussein as he led us back to the main road, Nineveh Street, where a square of bombed rubble opened out to our right. Blackened, mangled buildings stood proudly to one side, as if proclaiming defiance to the world and those who had bombed them. In the centre of the rubble, like a fountain in a town square, someone had placed a birdcage made of twisted scrap metal, and inside was a bird, black with a smudge of white, and a bright green water bowl. Alone, in the rubble. My heart stopped. Words failed me. They still do. In the midst of this destruction there was still a sense of hope, that not all was completely lost.

Bird cage in the ruins

Two brothers, both of them carpenters, had returned to set up shop on the edge of this wasteland. They had both fled during the war, one made it to the UK and the other to Norway. The UK sent Muhammad back to Iraq, but his brother managed to get Norwegian residency. At some point after ISIS had been expelled, he chose to return to Mosul and they were now making wooden bed frames which stood among the broken stones, lined up like orphans awaiting adoption.

The two brothers with with their bed frames

Hussein knew the men and they laughed as they spoke. Smiled and laughed. One brother had no choice but to come back to Iraq, but the other had chosen to leave a cold weather country of peace to return to the war zone which had once been his home and was, and still is, his culture. These two brothers touched something inside me, and even now as I write the tears are once again welling. Once more I am lost for words.

Hussein led us determinedly onwards, back into the ruins and out again, in and out, in and out. Past the remains of bombed churches and mosques - for ISIS had no compunction about destroying both. Of fourteen important Islamic sites listed on Wikipedia, only one was not destroyed by ISIS. And that is just the tip of the iceberg, there were many more. And many more churches too.

Less conspicuous, bodies are still being discovered under the rubble, and there are probably many more which may never be found.

The people's resilience was astonishing. We saw it in a mosque, badly damaged by ISIS but now under restoration as men worked together in a hive of activity to restore it to a functioning place of worship. They were motivated, proud to be contributing, and positive. Peter remembers the haunting image of a large upended dome, almost intact, yet inverted, blown there by the forces of dynamite. In its own way it was also an example of resilience.

Back on the main road Hussein was telling me that for some time after the bombings and destruction there had been no water and no electricity. The government was doing nothing to remedy the situation, so a local man had taken on the job himself, investing his own money in the project. Hussein was about to continue his story but abruptly stopped in mid-sentence when a young man appeared by our side, listening. Nodding to the man, we moved on in silence until, at a safe distance, Hussein explained that we were being watched, and must be careful what we said, for there were those who don't want the truth to be spoken. There were moments when I wondered where we were being led. Could we trust this man who'd picked us up in the fish market? Who was he really? Were we being too trusting, too naive? But my gut feeling was also telling me he was okay.

Following the river he took us to the Heritage Centre, a traditional old building, beautifully restored, where we met several extraordinary young people who were working or volunteering there. A young woman in her early twenties explained the collection of traditional tools and other items, as well as proudly showing us their virtual reality headsets which 'took' us on a tour of Hatra, an ancient fortified caravan city 110 kilometres southwest of Mosul. She had lived through the ISIS period as a teenager and spoke easily of her experience, of being unable to leave the home, and unable to attend school for three years. Yet her English was excellent. Fate had thrown adversity into her lap but she turned things on their head by using her time in enforced lockdown under ISIS to learn English. Online when possible. She was bubbly, cheerful, confident, and with full makeup Iraqi-style was absolutely gorgeous. And such a breath of fresh air in this world gone so horribly wrong - astonishingly full of positive thoughts, saying with confidence and passionate motivation that it's up to the youth of Mosul to change things and change them they will. Once again, this is Iraq.

We paused for a while by the river, gazing across its green banks as the water flowed by like rippling satin. A gentle breeze blew, birds flitted amongst the greenery and it was easy to imagine what a beautiful place this had been during times of peace, as the old city sloped down to the river banks, its tightly packed ancient buildings blending layer upon layer of history with the surroundings, and perhaps an old arched bridge in the distance. Now all gone. Paradise lost.

Far across the other side I could see the Mosul Grand Mosque rising like a complex jelly mould from the newer city, its central dome surrounded by many smaller domes atop rocket-shaped towers, all glowing in the sunshine. Saddam had started this huge bubbling creation which erupts above its surroundings, but construction was halted because of political instability and it remains unfinished.

With endless energy, Hussein led us up to the Bashtabiya, or Black Castle, overlooking the Tigris. The 12th-century castle had seen sieges and fighting over the centuries and, neglected after the 2003 invasion, was damaged by ISIS. Apart from two young *shebab* who rolled up on a motorbike, we were alone there and feeling a little unsure of the wisdom of blithely following our unknown man as he attempted to lure us down to the river bank. '*Come*' he shouted. '*It's a good place to rob you of your money.*' '*No*', we shouted back. And so it continued, '*Come*!' *No*', '*Come*!' *No*', '*Come*!', *No*' like a never ending volley in a tennis match. The *shebab*, who by now had climbed to the top of the ruins, were loving every minute of this verbal game and in the end we were all in hysterics. We finally gave in and followed Hussein down the slippery, gravelly slope. He didn't rob us, he didn't murder us, he just wanted to show us a hot spring.

Hussein[28] was loud, passionate, outspoken and at times bombastic, but he was also playful, cheekily naughty and had a quick sense of humour. He was quite a character, and by the time he led us back to the fish market we'd become rather fond of him and tipped him generously, in secret, inside a ruin, before waving goodbye. And oh what a merry walk he had taken us on! Looking back it seems we were fated to meet him there at the end of the fish market. Or was he waiting for us? Had the Mukhabarat[29] been alerted that we were on our way? This is Iraq, after all.

Keen to get back to Mosul before dark, we made it to the bus garage by the old walls of Nineveh in time, but had to wait for a minibus to fill up, finally leaving at 4.00 PM. On our way we stopped for twenty minutes on the main road, waiting for a young woman to join the bus, and not much further on a young *shebab* insisted on stopping to buy some crisps to munch on. This was fast becoming the bus trip from hell. To the left of the road we saw a convoy of military trucks heading slowly

---

[28] Not his real name

[29] Mukhabarat, secret police, literally, the hidden ones.

across the desert to the not so distant hills, and I remembered hearing that insurgents and ISIS were still hiding out there, only emerging after dark. The sun was setting as we arrived at the border checkpoint, in the middle of nowhere. The Kurdish official glared towards me and Peter, asking what our relationship was and in controlled fury Peter spat back that I was his sister. I think it was at this point that Peter's calm finally cracked, as he exploded with a passionate declaration that he was fed up with checkpoints and being picked on. Not long after that, in a sudden rush all the *shebab* left the bus to have their luggage checked, and our driver took off. Either he was fed up or they were going somewhere else. Peter suspected they were jettisoned like the cargo of a sinking ship to give the rest of us a better chance of survival! I wondered if they were heading for the hills to join the insurgents. I don't know, but from then on it was another drive on the wild side, into a magnificent sunset of ever deepening reds until full darkness descended. We had vowed never to travel on these roads after dark, but there we were. It was hell. It was also a huge relief to see the sparkling lights of Erbil ahead.

After a day swirling with the most intense emotions, at the end of it all I can only say that I'd do it all again. It was like coming back to life after hibernating in the comfort of modern, secure Erbil.

***

Top: Hussein walking in the old city
Bottom: The Mosul Grand Mosque across the river

Top: Remains of a home in the rubble
Bottom: 'Safe' building in old Mosul

11

EPILOGUE

20 March 2023 and the internet is full of articles about the twentieth anniversary of the US/UK invasion of Iraq and the tragic legacy left for the long suffering people of Iraq.

In my month of wandering through Iraq and meeting a thousand and one people I never raised questions about that war. I didn't need to. Some offered matter of fact stories of their losses, without looking for sympathy. Others spoke of knowing endless war, nothing but war, and many regretted the demise of Saddam. A dentist spoke bitterly about the lack of equipment, remembering the excellent medical services available before the west imposed sanctions on the country, destroying the once first class medical system. Others recalled the heyday of cultural activity in the 1970s, with investment in culture, theatre, art, and education. Under Saddam. Many talked about the present corruption, and lack of investment in restoring broken infrastructure, hospitals and schools. Of course in oil rich Iraq there should be no lack of money. Were it not for corruption.

We glimpsed the dark underbelly of the country, the side effects of poverty and war in visions of decay and destruction. We saw the mess and debris, broken people missing a leg or an arm, and at times we felt it, as an undercurrent in streets abandoned to rot in apocalyptic horror.

War, slaughter, destruction - the story of Iraq's long history.

And yet, side by side with this there lives hope, resilience, determination, courage and a culture rich with a spectacular generosity and welcoming spirit. After all the people have suffered at the hands of foreign powers, how is that possible? Simply put, this is Iraq.

Time and again Iraqis refused payment for food and drinks with the cry of 'This is Iraq!', their generosity like no other I've ever encountered. 'This is Iraq' became an everyday mantra, for the razor-wire spilling out from unexpected places, the endless invitations for lunch, the kindness of people feeding street dogs, the joyful exuberance of the people. And of course the magnificent heritage left by ancient civilisations. Iraq and everyday Iraqis are quite simply astonishing. It is a country where passing back and forth through the looking glass becomes normal, moving between the ancient and the modern, from the kind and generous to late afternoon danger, from smiling militia to sudden skirmishes.

Iraq is not a country for those seeking the cliched pleasures of stunning landscapes, colourful beauty and comfort offered by the usual destinations of mass tourism. No, Iraq has none of that gloss of superficiality. It's raw, it's tough and it's real. Its mostly flat and desert-dry landscape stretches from north to south, monotonous in shades of beige and grey. Its cities are ladled with dust and war-torn decay, the air heavy with the lingering toxins of war. The aridity is occasionally punctuated by splashes of greenery - in the Marshes of the south, and by the ribbons of greenery which follow the Euphrates and Tigris. Shadowing these green ribbons lie the ruins of fallen empires, rich with a legacy of 4,000 years of civilisation. But beyond the richness and magnificence of the past, it is the people who offer the most precious of lessons. Of survival, resilience, determination and a generous hospitality. Despite everything.

*

On our last evening in Iraq, in Erbil, we dined on excellent, succulent kebabs as we perched by the roadside on unstable chairs, watching the cook flourishing kebab skewers like swords as the traffic surged by, while a passing man seemed to be talking to the gods as he pointed his head skywards.

And that night Peter read me Chapter Seven of Sinbad the Sailor, the final chapter of my bedside stories which had begun in Basrah, for we were leaving early the following morning.

*

The inspiration which gave rise to the Ziggurat of Ur, the Malwiya Minaret, Babylon, and the fabulous voyages of Sindbad the Sailor did not spring from nowhere. There is magic in this part of the world, and it lingers still.

Iraq is a thousand and one worlds away from the commercialisation of life in the cocooned, easy comfort of the western world where senses are dulled and values are trivialised.

I have never felt so alive as I did in Iraq, where days lived so close to a knife-edge added a much deeper perspective to the meaning of being alive.

*

Peter left on the 3.45 AM flight to Cairo.

I left two hours later for Istanbul.

Heartbroken to leave.

Twas it all but a dream?

***

A FEW WORDS ABOUT PETER

Without Peter I would probably never have gone to Iraq, and without his knowledge of Arabic the experience would have been less enriching. We looked out for each other, had a thousand and one laughs along the way, and there's nobody else in this world who would have lulled me to sleep with tales of Sindbad the Sailor.

When it came to putting this adventure together on paper, Peter not only brilliantly edited the text for its many mistakes, but he also pointed out what was missing and added great chunks of details too. His memory is far better than mine.

So a huge thank you to my friend, editor and partner in travel to far-flung, off-the-beaten-track places.... Syria, Yemen, Pakistan, Bangladesh and Iraq, not to mention more obscure parts of Jordan and India ....

Where shall we go next?

***

In the Shabandar Cafe

CAPTIONS AND PHOTO CREDITS

Cover: Haydar-Khana Mosque (Deborah Williams)
Back cover: Peter and Deborah, (Deborah Williams)

4	At the Iraq Border (Deborah Williams)
5	Dome in old souq (Deborah Williams)
6	We Deserve Life, on Sadoun Street (Deborah Williams)
21	*Tawla* and tea in the Umm Kalthum cafe (Deborah Williams)
23	Haydar-Khana Mosque on Al Rasheed Street (Deborah Williams)
23	Sagging old building in old Baghdad (Deborah Williams)
27	Military apparel fit for the Carnivale (Deborah Williams)
28	Mr Bean gazing down on Al Rasheed Street (Deborah Williams)
29	Apocalyptic side-street off Sadoun Street (Deborah Williams)
33	Baghdad Train Station (Deborah Williams)
34	Cathedral-like interior, Baghdad Train Station (Deborah Williams)
42	400-year-old khan in souq (Deborah Williams)
43	Detail on minaret, old Baghdad (Deborah Williams)
44	Glittering interior of Karbala shrine (Deborah Williams)
56	The airy Great Mosque of Kufa (Deborah Williams)
58	Woman on cart, Jumhurya Street (Deborah Williams)
59	Wall panel inside the Kufa Mosque (Deborah Williams)

60	Babylon's mythical Mushussu (Deborah Williams)
60	Aurochs and Mushussu marching across Babylon's ancient walls (Deborah Williams)
69	Saddam's Palace overlooking the ruins of Babylon (Deborah Williams)
69	Graffitied walls inside Saddam's Palace (Deborah Williams)
70	Ziggurat of Ur, looming large (Deborah Williams)
70	Stairway to the gods, Ziggurat of Ur (Deborah Williams)
78	Three Happy Travellers (Peter D. Musgrove)
81	Flying High on the Ziggurat (Nick Cornwall)
82	Reed construction (Deborah Williams)
83	Inside a Mudhif (Deborah Williams)
84	Mudhifs in the Marshes (Deborah Williams)
86	Gathering reeds in the Marshes (Deborah Williams)
87	Buffalo and shelter in the Marshes (Deborah Williams)
87	'Tea cosy' engines (Deborah Williams)
88	Ceiling in old house, Basrah (Deborah Williams)
91	Sheikh Khazaal Mansion under restoration (Deborah Williams)
92	Shanasheel houses catching the breeze (Deborah Williams)
92	Doorway in old Basrah (Deborah Williams)
97	Street-side fish barbecue (Deborah Williams)
101	On the platform, Basrah Train Station (Deborah Williams)
102	Early morning, Malwiya Minaret (Deborah Williams)
111	Mini-replica Malwiya Minaret at the crossroads (Deborah Williams)

112	Front of Ctesiphon Arch (Deborah Williams)
112	The Arch, close up (Deborah Williams)
117	Peter with the Great Crested Grebe (Deborah Williams)
118	Rusting land mine warning (Deborah Williams)
123	Dwarfed by the Ctesiphon Arch (Deborah Williams)
124	Side view of leaning front wall (Deborah Williams)
124	Walls beyond thick (Deborah Williams)
125	At the Salman Pak checkpoint (Deborah Williams)
126	Choli Minaret, Erbil (Deborah Williams)
134	The Citadel, overshadowing old Erbil (Deborah Williams)
142	Back street in old Erbil (Deborah Williams)
143	Spiderman and fairy floss in the square below the Citadel (Deborah Williams)
144	Ruins of Mosul's once-beautiful old city (Deborah Williams)
150	Bird cage in the ruins (Deborah Williams)
151	The two brothers with their bed frames (Deborah Williams)
157	Hussein walking in in the old city (Deborah Williams)
157	The Mosul Grand Mosque across the river (Deborah Williams)
158	Remains of a home in the rubble (Deborah Williams)
158	'Safe' building in old Mosul (Deborah Williams)
163	Peter in the Shabandar Cafe (Deborah Williams)
167	In the Marshes (Peter D. Musgrove)

ABOUT THE AUTHOR

Born in Melbourne, Australia, Deborah inherited from her father an obsession with movement, travel and adventure, and from her mother, a sense of the ridiculous and a long-lasting delight in eccentric beings. She has spent the greater part of her life wandering the less touristed areas of the world, mostly in Asia and the Middle East, and is increasingly in search of the old ways and all those things we have lost to the relentless march of modernity.

Based in France, she is the author of *'Lunch in Lahore, Dinner in Delhi: Travels with the Diaries of a WW2 Bomber Pilot'*, which traces her father's wartime footsteps as a bomber pilot with the RAAF from England to India.

Contact: debwilliamsau@gmail.com

***

In the Marshes

Printed in Great Britain
by Amazon